All About
the Weather

allabout
books

by Ivan Ray Tannehill

Senior Meteorologist, U.S. Weather Bureau

Illustrated by Rene Martin

RANDOM HOUSE
NEW YORK

To my three grandchildren

Ric, John and Jane

Table of Contents

Foreword

In our lifetime we will see many new and exciting developments in science—probably more than in any previous period in the world's history. Some of these will be in the field of meteorology—the study of the weather. Even now we can see the beginnings of startling new things in weather science.

This is important to everybody. For no matter what you do, the weather is one of the big influences in your life. The better you understand it the more surely you will find it working for you instead of against you.

All About the Weather tells you the story of weather in simple language but with scientific accuracy. It has been written by the man who has headed the program of

Foreword

reporting and forecasting in the United States Weather Bureau for many years and has studied the weather around the globe. Here he tells the story of weather as it affects the people of the earth. He tells how weathermen predict storms, floods, blizzards or just "fair and warmer." He tells of man's struggle to defend himself against the huge forces of the atmosphere when they are turned against him.

Man has already made a beginning in the control of the weather in a small and very limited way. For many other reasons, too, the weather and the work weathermen do is becoming more and more important to the growing populations of the earth. As our transportation speeds up and as industry and commerce grow, so do the demands for information about the weather. It is no wonder that people in every land are asking to know "all about the weather!" In this book one of the best-known weathermen in the world gives a weather report that is exciting because it is true.

Francis W. Reichelderfer
Chief, U.S. Weather Bureau
Washington, D.C.

1.

The Weatherman Predicts a Storm

Weather is the thing we talk about most. When it is very hot or very cold, very wet or very dry, the weather enters into every conversation. And when a big storm comes along, we talk about little else. "Where did this awful weather come from?" we repeat over and over again.

Often it seems as if the storm came out of nowhere.

It may be a clear, cold day in winter. We see nothing in the air. Suddenly we notice long, gray clouds spreading across the sky. Soft snow begins to fall, covering the leafless branches and gathering on streets, roofs and sidewalks. The wind rises. Blowing around street corners and making white streaks across the fields, the storm whistles in the wires and roars in the eaves. Snow piles against buildings and fences.

Next day we read that we aren't the only ones who caught it. We are in the line of a great storm which is moving across the country. Throughout the Northeast, traffic is tied up because of snow. In the West there was a blizzard—snow and high winds and temperatures below zero. We learn that thousands of livestock have perished because their owners didn't heed the storm warning in time to get them under cover. A number of motorists were caught on the roads and their cars were almost buried in the drifts.

Shaking our heads over the news, we go out to shovel the walk.

Or perhaps it is a hot night in summer. There is no hint of a breeze. Heated air is trapped in the bedrooms. We lie sleepless on our beds, expecting it to be unbearably hot most of the night. And suddenly there is a rumble of thunder rolling from cloud to cloud. We look outside and see the reflection of lightning in the windows of the house across the street. As we look, big drops of rain hit the side of the house, and a gust of wind sets the curtains dancing.

"Is it possible that out of this quiet night a great storm has been born?" we ask ourselves.

Cooler air comes with a second gust of wind. Then a blinding flash of lightning tells us we must close the windows. As we get up to do it, a great roar of thunder and a deluge of rain frighten us a little. Suddenly hail beats against the windows. Flashes of lightning reveal trees bent low and torn leaves racing in the wind.

A blizzard may bring snow drifts deep enough to bury a car.

"What demon of the night has come to visit us?" we ask. The power of the storm holds us in awe.

Later on we learn that this was not a single storm. There was a long line of storms reaching hundreds of miles across the land. Some were very destructive. Hail did great damage to fruit trees and crops in the fields. In some places there were tornadoes. People huddled in storm cellars while buildings were broken to bits, cows and horses were carried away by the wind, and orchards were uprooted.

Lying on our beds in the heat, we knew nothing about what was coming. But the weatherman knew. He sent out warnings. At the airport they took precautions at once. When the warning came over the teletype, men hurried right out and tied the planes down. An air liner that had already gone up circled around overhead and changed its course. It wasn't going to get in the way of that storm! Oh no!

How did the weatherman know that a storm was coming?

Well, it certainly wasn't because he went out to view the sky and didn't like the way the moon looked or the way the stars twinkled. He knew about the storm long before sunset. And it wasn't because his joints ached or his corns throbbed. His feet were sound, and his joints didn't ache. Nor was it because soot fell down the chimney. No. He didn't resort to any of these old-fashioned signs to tell him a storm was brewing. He had far better ways of predicting the weather.

In part he knew a change in the weather was coming because there was a change in the temperature and in the wind and in the moisture in the air. To him the storm wasn't sudden. It was an orderly change. It gave warning of what was going to happen.

Yet the weatherman could never have understood the full meaning of Nature's warning if many others hadn't helped him. Even if he had spent his whole life observing the weather, he could never have understood it from his observations alone.

For what we know about weather comes from thousands of observers in many countries. We have learned about weather from men who have kept records on every continent. We have learned from men who have probed the Arctic and Antarctic. We have learned from those who ventured into the deserts of Asia and the wilds of Africa. Perhaps most of all we have learned from observers on ships at sea. For three-fourths of the surface of our planet is water. Our knowledge of the great storms of the sea came first of all from men who experienced those storms. They observed what happened as they clung to the decks of sailing ships in hurricane winds and mountainous seas. Afterwards they took time to make notes of what they saw.

Putting all these observations together, we have slowly come to realize that our weather isn't something apart from the weather of the world. We have learned that the air around our earth doesn't stand still and that its huge motions carry the weather from place to place. We have learned that our weather of tomorrow and the next day is sweeping toward us today from distant parts. Storms are seldom a surprise to the weatherman because he knows when storms are on the way. He knows when they are getting near. He takes into consideration not only his own observations but also all the reports he gets. On the basis of these he makes his prediction.

No, the weatherman doesn't have to see if his joints ache or his corns throb to know what the weather is going to do. He doesn't have to go to the groundhog or the cuckoo or the donkey to tell him what's going to happen. Millions of weather records have proved that human beings who observe and keep records are much more dependable guides.

Some clouds look as if they have been painted with a brush.

To be sure, there are some old weather signs and sayings that sometimes hit the mark. For instance, an old Indian proverb says that "When the sun is in his house, it will rain soon." That is a poetic way of saying that when there is a halo around the sun, there will be rain. Now and again the sign is a true weather prophet, but often it misses.

Another hit-and-miss saying goes like this:

"Trace in the sky the painter's brush;

The winds around you soon will rush."

The meaning of these lines is that high, thin clouds

spreading across the sky and showing bright colors at sunset are a sign of stormy weather. Well, sometimes they are. But then, again, they aren't.

The main trouble with such signs is that they say nothing about the causes of the changes in the weather and so add little or nothing to our understanding of what is going on. That understanding is growing all the time. The more observers we have, the more records are kept, the more we learn. And the more we learn, the better the weatherman can predict the weather.

Sometimes there seems to be a halo around the sun.

2.

Our Invisible Ocean of Air

Outside the tropics, weather never stays the same very long. It is always changing, always becoming something different. Several times a day we look out to see what the weather is doing. For be there wind or rain or snow or a glorious sunny day with fleecy clouds in a blue sky, we know it is just a passing mood of the atmosphere.

What is this atmosphere whose moods affect our lives so much? We can't see it, we can't touch it. It has no color, no odor. Yet we know that it is there. We become aware of it every time we hear the rustle of leaves in the treetops, whenever we see trees bow down before the wind. We sense then that a play is going on around us—a play on an invisible stage, often with invisible actors.

Sometimes we realize with a start that because of that atmosphere we are like fish at the bottom of a deep, deep ocean. Only our ocean of air isn't confined to a basin. It flows continuously all the way around the earth and stretches up, up to heights many times deeper than the Pacific. Down at the bottom of the watery depths of the ocean, it is black night everlasting. Nature has to provide the fish of the lower depths with lanterns so they can see their way around. But we can look straight up through our ocean of air. We can see the sun by day and the moon and the stars by night.

This ocean of air is transparent because it is made up of a mixture of invisible gases. A little more than three quarters of the atmosphere is composed of nitrogen. Not quite one quarter is oxygen. Only one part in a hundred is made up of other gases, and of that small part argon forms all but a tiny fraction.

As everybody knows, gases don't weigh much. As "light as air," we say. But that doesn't mean that the atmosphere has no weight. It means only that we don't feel the weight of the miles and miles of air pressing down on us. Our bodies have adjusted themselves to bearing that weight just as the bodies of the fish in the miles-deep ocean are adjusted to bearing the weight of water above them.

Well, how much pressure do we bear?

Not nearly as much as the fish of the lower depths.

At the earth's surface air weighs 1/800 as much as an equal volume of water. That doesn't seem much. But when all the miles of air above us are accounted for, we find that air has a good deal of weight. It presses down on us almost fifteen pounds on every square inch.

Now one of the curious things about gases is that they have no shape and no size. If you take a jar and pour a little water in it, the water will stay in the bottom of the jar. You can't do that with air. You can't fill a jar part way with air—or with any other gases—because gases will take up as much room as you give them. Gases expand. Why then doesn't the atmosphere expand all the way up to the moon? Or the stars? Why doesn't it take up all the space there is?

The answer is that it can't. Everything in Nature obeys the laws of Nature. But sometimes two laws operate against each other. The law of gases is that they expand. But, like every other form of matter, gases have to obey the law of gravity as well. The earth pulls the atmosphere toward itself just as it pulls us toward itself. And that is the reason, of course, why after three billion years there is still air around the earth. Luckily for us our planet has held on tight to its atmosphere. If not for that, we wouldn't have had a chance. The earth would be like the moon, which has lost its atmosphere—a dead and barren world. And no human being would be there to see how dismal it was. For we can live many days without food, a few days without water, but only minutes without air.

Why is that?

It is so because, though we seldom stop to think about it, we are wholly dependent on the invisible ocean of air above us. Our bodies are adjusted to living on its bottom. Our lungs breathe in oxygen to oxidize or burn up the waste products in our blood. And the plants on which we and the herb-eating animals feed depend on the atmosphere's carbon dioxide for their needs. We take oxygen from the air and breathe out carbon dioxide. Plants do just the opposite. They take in carbon dioxide and give oxygen back to the air.

So it's a lucky thing that the atmosphere has to obey

the law of gravity as well as the law of expansion. Air expands, but not enough to get away from us.

There's another thing about that expansion. Air doesn't expand evenly. The higher up it is, the thinner our atmosphere gets, and the lower down, the denser it is. That's because air responds to pressure. The air presses on us, but it also presses down on itself. Every layer presses down on every other layer, just as books in a pile press down on those underneath. The total

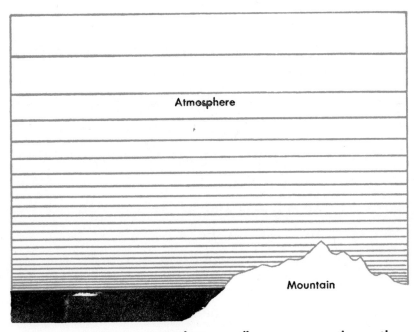

Layers of air are squeezed into smaller space near the earth.

weight of that pressure is a great deal, for it is estimated that the atmosphere around the earth weighs some 5,900 trillions of tons. So down near the earth the air gets squeezed into smaller space. It is packed down so hard that more than half of all the atmosphere is in the lowest 3½ miles. The first 18 miles above the earth contain 97 percent of all the atmosphere.

But how far up does it go? If not as far as the moon, how far does the atmosphere extend?

We aren't sure. There is no upper surface to our ocean of air the way there is an upper surface to the oceans of water. But we have learned something about it from shooting stars. Everything that passes near the earth is drawn toward it. The wandering masses of stone or metal which we call meteorites respond to that irresistible pull of the earth. They come tearing down through the atmosphere, and as they do so the friction with the air makes them burn. We can see them burning at heights ranging from 40 to 200 miles. So we know there is air that far up.

We have learned something from watching the aurora, too. One of the wonders of the polar regions, the aurora borealis is now known to be an electrical action of the sun on the upper atmosphere. We can see the northern lights as high as 700 miles up. So we know there must be air—however thin—up that high. Perhaps there is air still farther up. Perhaps there are widely spaced particles of air even a thousand miles up and higher.

The aurora shows streamers, bands, curtains or arcs of light.

3.

Five Thousand Miles Up

Nowadays there is a great deal of talk about rocket ships that will go zooming through space from planet to planet. A journey on such a ship certainly would give us a close-up view of our atmosphere. So let us imagine that we can actually take off on a space ship. Let us start, say, from Cleveland, Ohio.

It is a hot July day. Everywhere over the city the temperature is above 90° except on the shore of Lake Erie where the cool water keeps the air down to 86°. Everybody is panting. It seems we are very far away from any place where the weather would be cold. Around the curve of the lake at Toledo, 100 miles away, it is just as hot as in Cleveland. In every other direction it is the same. How will we find things in the air above?

Rising in our imaginary rocket ship, we slant off toward the southwest. For we want to be above the center of the country. As we go up, we notice almost at once that the air is getting cooler. Every 300 feet we move upward, the temperature drops one degree. By the time we are two miles up, it is almost down to 50°—overcoat temperature. With a start we realize that cold weather wasn't so very far away after all. In the direction of the sky it was almost at hand. We pass through scattered clouds now. Through the openings between them we look back at the city and the lake spread out behind us. It seems odd to think that people are suffocating down there.

Up, up we go. In our imaginary ship we are now above five miles. That's about even with the peaks of the highest mountains in the world. "No wonder," we think, "that Mont Blanc and Mt. Everest are covered with snow the year around!" Outside our ship the temperature is 20° below zero and falling steadily. Here we are above most of the clouds and storms in the world. A few thin white swirls stretch across the sky above us like cobwebs. We shall soon leave them behind, too.

We think of climbers with instruments on their backs toiling up steep mountain sides to find out, among other things, what temperatures are like at those awful heights. We think of courage and risk, of lives lost in avalanches and deep crevasses, of endless endurance and heroism. Ours is a much easier way of finding out. In moments we can reach heights that took them days and weeks to attain.

We are up above the highest mountains now. Our observations tell us that great gales are blowing around us. We are in the jet stream of the upper air. The wind is nearly 200 miles an hour. On earth we call any wind that blows at more than 75 miles an hour a hurricane. If this wind were down on the earth, it would be causing terrible destruction. Whole regions would be devastated.

Still we rise. And now at 8 miles we find that the wind has suddenly ceased. The temperature is around 68° below zero.

How much colder is it going to get? We watch the instruments carefully and are thrilled to see that the temperature now stands still. We live over again one of the most startling discoveries in meteorology, the science of weather.

Until the beginning of this century, scientists thought the air continued to get colder all the way to the end of the atmosphere. They were amazed when balloons carrying weather instruments high over Europe from 1899 to 1902 showed that this wasn't true. The instruments recorded that at about 7 or 8 miles the temperature begins to stand still and remains that way for the next several miles.

Some of our fliers are very well acquainted with this strange region which we call the *stratosphere*. But for most of us the *troposphere*, as the region closest to the earth is called, is much more important. It is in the troposphere that most of the drama of the weather takes place.

Well, we are moving fast through the stratosphere and although the temperature stands still, we are satisfied. After all, 68° below zero is a quite respectable cold. We wouldn't have believed that such a short distance away from Cleveland and only 7 or 8 miles up we would find cold like the cold of Arctic winter.

Now we have gone 15 miles into the air. We are up

as high as man has ventured into the upper atmosphere. That was in a rocket plane. We see now the black sky described by men who have gone high up in balloons. We are thrilled to see the heavens filled with stars. We clearly see them although it is daytime. The sun shines fiercely. We see its pearly corona, something that we have beheld on earth only when there was an eclipse of the sun. The air up here is so thin it doesn't produce a blue color for the sky or hide the stars or the sun's corona.

We are still shooting upward through the stratosphere, and now another curious experience awaits us. Up around thirty miles it is warm again. At that height, scientists have found out, it is sometimes warmer than on the hottest days down at the surface of the earth!

It was very startling for them to learn this. Scientists had always thought that it would get colder right up to the top of the atmosphere. Then something set them wondering. In 1901 when Queen Victoria of England died, the ceremonies of her funeral included the firing of great cannon. The noise of the firing was heard near by and also at distant places. But in between there were places where the sound wasn't heard. What made the silent zones? It was puzzling. Scientists who studied

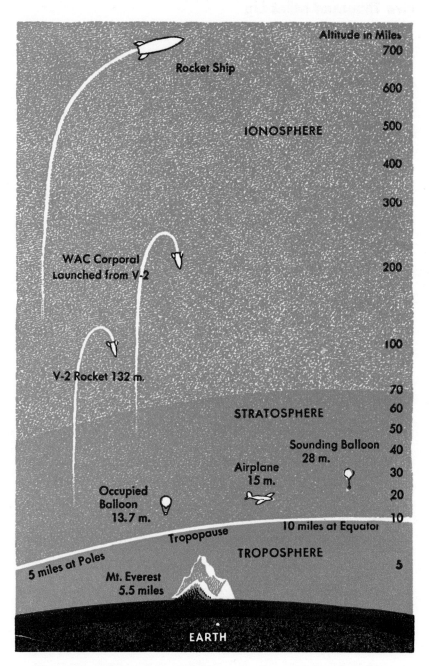

Altitude in Miles

Rocket Ship

700

600

IONOSPHERE 500

400

300

WAC Corporal
Launched from V-2 200

V-2 Rocket 132 m. 100

70

STRATOSPHERE 60
50
Sounding Balloon
28 m. 40
Airplane
15 m. 30
Occupied
Balloon 20
13.7 m.
10
10 miles at Equator
Tropopause

5 miles at Poles TROPOSPHERE 5

Mt. Everest
5.5 miles

EARTH

The atmosphere as it might be seen from our rocket ship.

the reports of the funeral concluded later on that the sound of firing heard at the distant places was refracted sound. It was sound bent back from a warm layer in the high atmosphere.

Rocket data leave no doubt about that now. There is heat in the high atmosphere. That heat is due to the presence of ozone, which is a form of oxygen. There is a layer of ozone up there made by the action of the sun's ultraviolet rays on ordinary oxygen. And a good thing for us that the layer of ozone is up there to protect us! For though a little ultraviolet is good for us, in large amounts those rays would kill us. If not for that layer of ozone, we would be in serious trouble.

Well, now we are nearing the top of the stratosphere and we find that the temperature has fallen again. At 50 miles it is nearly as cold as at the bottom of the stratosphere.

Is it going to get colder from now on out?

On the contrary. We are in the region of the sky from which radio waves are reflected back to earth. Here in the *ionosphere* we are in for some more surprises.

In the layer between 50 and 60 miles up, the temperature begins to rise again. This time it goes extremely high. Is it possible that we read 1,000°?

Scientists aren't sure what causes this great heat. It may be due to oxygen absorbing some of the sun's short rays. It is hard to tell. But one thing we know. The great heat up here doesn't seem to mean much to our weather down below. The air up here is extremely thin.

The air, of course, has been getting thinner all the time. In the layer above 70 miles it is more than 100,000 times as thin as at the surface of the earth. But as we go shooting farther out, the air becomes incredibly thin. It almost ceases to exist. The gas particles are very, very far apart.

And still we go zooming upward. At 5,000 miles our imaginary ship has reached the end of its outward force and is slowing down. Now it is tilting over with the ship's nose toward the earth. The downward plunge begins. We look toward the earth, and a wonderful sight is before us. We behold our planet as the space man of the future will see it!

There it is with its belts of weather and storms moving across the face of the earth. Hazy and broken here and there, the belts extend east and west around our planet. Around the middle there is the calm belt called the *doldrums*, where in the days of sailing ships mari-

Weather belts as they would look 5,000 miles above the earth.

ners were often becalmed. It shows white where the clouds reflect the sun's rays. The regions of the trade winds to either side are spotted here and there with clouds over the continents, but over the oceans these wind belts show as two dark strips. Farther away from the equator big white patches mark the storm areas.

This being summer in our hemisphere, the North Pole is turned toward the sun. We can see there is not much snow and ice in the far north at this season. Far to the south the Antarctic region is hidden behind the bulge of the earth at the equator. Otherwise we might see a vast patch of white in that direction.

The earth is getting larger and larger, and now we can no longer see it as a globe. Soon our journey is almost over. In no time at all we have ripped through the clouds of the troposphere. And here we are. We are back in prostrated Cleveland. We check the temperature. It is still above 90°.

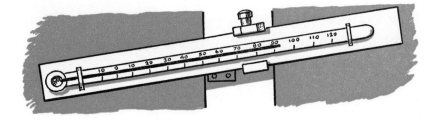

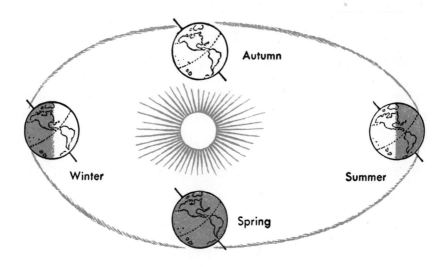

4.

Sun, Earth and Wind

People often say, "Everything depends on the weather." But what does the weather depend on? Why do we have weather at all?

Behind all our weather—behind the warm summer days and the cold winter days, behind the winds, behind the rain, behind the storms—is the sun. The sun is not only the source of all our life but also of all our weather. To understand why this is so we need first of all to get some idea of the tremendous heat which the sun sends out in all directions.

The sun is extremely hot. Astronomers tell us that the temperature at the sun's surface must be measured in thousands of degrees. In the interior the sun's heat must be measured in millions of degrees. Such temperatures are too high for the mind to grasp—they make all our earthly heats seem lukewarm. It is a good thing we are 93 million miles away from the sun and get only a tiny fraction of the rays it sends out!

Now as everybody knows, our planet spins at a terrific speed around this tremendously hot sun. At the same time every 24 hours the earth turns completely around on its axis. As it turns, each part of the earth's surface is brought toward and then away from the sun. We say the sun rises and sets, but it is the earth turning on its axis. This turning brings a change of temperature from day to night. It causes some of the daily changes in our weather.

But there are the seasonal changes, too—winter and summer, spring and fall. What brings them about?

Two things. In part the changes have to do with the path the earth takes around the sun. In part they have to do with the way the earth is tilted.

It's like this. The earth's path around the sun is not a perfect circle. Nor is the sun exactly in the center.

In summer the sun is high in the sky. Its rays beat down on us.

This means that in one part of the path the earth is nearer the sun than in the opposite part. You would think that this would happen in our summer. But no. Strangely it is in our winter that this occurs. In our winter the earth is nearer the sun than in our summer.

Why, then, isn't it warmer in our winter than in our summer?

It would be except for one thing. If the earth weren't tilted at an angle, it really would be warmer in our winter than in our summer. That slanting of the earth's axis makes all the difference.

In summer our hemisphere is turned *toward* the sun. In winter, when the earth is on the opposite side of the

Sun

Winter

In winter the same sun rays must heat a larger area.

path, our hemisphere is turned *away* from the sun. So, although in summer we are farther away from the sun, its rays reach us more directly. The sun beats right down on us instead of coming at an angle, and so it gives us more heat than in winter when it is low in the sky.

In spring and fall the earth's axis is pointed neither toward nor away from the sun but off to the side. This gives us less heat than in summer and more than in winter. For this reason the weather generally is mild in spring and fall, neither very hot nor very cold.

But there is something else that happens as the earth travels around—its own surface, heated by the sun's rays, starts to give off heat. The earth warms the layer of air closest to it. And that starts a whole chain of events. The winds are born. Yes, the winds that are so large a part of weather and that bring so much of our weather to us start 'way back with the heating of the earth's surface by the sun.

Nobody has ever seen the wind. We certainly can feel it when we have to hold on to our hats. We can see what it does to the trees. We stand in awe when it dashes great waves upon the shore. We take advantage of the wind's power to make windmills whirl and sailboats move. When we put up high buildings and bridges we take the wind's force into account. But we cannot see the wind.

What is it? What is this invisible force we call the wind?

Wind is air in motion. The faster the air is moving, the stronger the wind is.

But what makes the air move?

That can't be answered in a word or a sentence. We can start by saying that wind is caused partly by the fact that land and water, and therefore the air next to them, are not heated and cooled equally. Land heats quickly and cools quickly. Water heats slowly and cools slowly.

This means that when the sun sends down its rays

and heats the earth, the land gets warmer than the water. The air next to the land becomes warmer than the air next to the water. Warm air expands and becomes light— its particles are farther apart. Cool air is more compact and heavy. So there is a difference in pressure. The cool air presses down more heavily than the warm air. And that's what starts the air moving.

For the law of winds is this: air close to the earth tries to move from regions where there is more pressure to regions where there is less pressure. It tries to, but many things interfere and it takes on a spiral motion, as we shall see later on. Or, as the weatherman says, air moves out of and around regions of *high* pressure and into and around regions of *low* pressure.

People who live near the seashore profit by this law in hot summer weather. During the day they get a nice, cool sea breeze. The air over the sea is cool. The air over the land is hot. The hot air is pushed upward, and the cool air from the sea comes in to take its place. People living as far as ten, twenty, even thirty miles inland may feel the breeze.

At night things happen just the other way around. The land cools more rapidly than the water. So in the night or early morning a breeze starts blowing

During the day there is usually a cool breeze from the sea.

in the other direction—from the land to the sea.

The same thing works on a bigger scale, too. Whole continents become warm in summer. Oceans are not so warm. The wind blows from sea to land. In winter it happens just the other way. The cold air next to the surface of the continent moves toward the sea. This is how the great monsoons of Asia operate. They blow in warm and wet from the ocean in summer; they blow out cold and dry from the land in winter.

The sun is behind everything. Both because it heats land and water unequally and for other reasons, it causes

At night a breeze starts blowing from the land to the sea.

the air to circulate. Over vast areas the winds blow steadily, changing from season to season.

The giant motions of the earth also play a part. As the earth hurries around its path at 18½ miles a second and spins on its axis like a top—1,000 miles an hour at the equator—the sun changes its daily circle in the sky. The atmosphere is stirred by the changes in heat caused by these motions. And the winds blow. Now they blow softly, now with gale force.

In the hot belt around the equator the warm air is pushed up. From both sides, north and south, cooler air moves toward the equator in steady streams. These are the trade winds.

Farther away from the equator are the belts of prevailing westerlies. Here the winds are moving eastward and toward the poles. This is most important for us because the United States is in the northern belt of prevailing westerlies. Our weather is the changing kind which comes with the winds in this belt.

Still farther from the equator, in the cold regions around the poles, the air is heavy. So it often moves toward the equator. There is continuous movement in the atmosphere. There is continuous circulation of air.

Air moves out of regions of high pressure and into regions of low. It tries to move directly, but actually it is carried off in a curve or, as we say, *deflected*. Because the earth is always turning, anything loose on its surface which starts to move from one point to another never reaches the point toward which it started. For by the time it moves that far, the earth has turned under it and carried away the place for which it was heading.

That's how it is with the winds. Any wind that starts toward the equator is turned to the right in our hemisphere and to the left in the southern hemisphere. Thus the trade winds are not north and south winds but northeast and southeast winds. They are turned to the right in our hemisphere and to the left in the southern hemisphere.

But that's only part of the story. Air doesn't always move with the same speed. It's just the way it is with water flowing from one level to another. The greater the difference in level, the faster the water flows. So with wind. The greater the difference in pressure between the high and the low, the faster the wind blows.

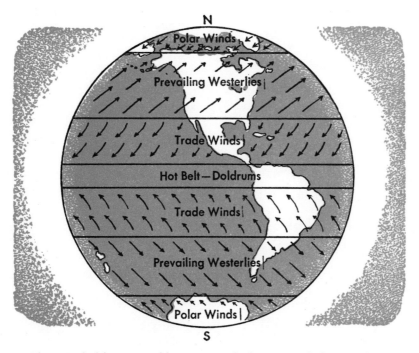

The winds blow steadily in great belts around the earth.

Can we tell how fast the wind is blowing?

Yes, and without any instruments at all. All we have to do is use our eyes. For moving air will press against any object in its path. We make many a use of that fact. Our windmills and sails work on that principle. We also make use of it in determining wind direction. We put a weather vane on top of a roof or a steeple. The wind blows against the broad vane and points the arrow in one direction or another.

The weather vane will not tell us the velocity of the wind, of course. But because we know that moving air will press against any object in its path, we can roughly measure how fast the wind is blowing. All we need do is look out the window and watch the effect the wind has on surrounding objects. There is a scale which helps us judge the wind's speed. This scale was first made to use on the sea to judge the wind by its effects on sails. But it has been adapted for use on land. It is given here in a simple form. It is a good idea to copy it and tack it up in a handy place to refer to.

What to Observe	Miles per Hour	Kind of Wind
Smoke goes straight up; Flags hang limp	0	Calm
Smoke drifts a little and shows wind direction	1–3	Slight
Wind felt on face; Leaves rustle	4–7	Light breeze
Leaves move constantly; Flags stand out	8–12	Gentle breeze
Small branches sway; Dust begins to blow	13–18	Moderate wind
Small trees in leaf begin to sway	19–24	Fresh wind
Large branches sway; Whistling heard in wires; Umbrellas hard to hold	25–31	Strong wind
Whole trees in motion; Not easy to walk against wind	32–38	High wind
Breaks twigs off trees; Walking very difficult	39–46	Gale
Slight damage to buildings; Breaks branches off trees	47–54	Strong gale
Trees uprooted; Breaks windows	55–63	Whole gale
Widespread damage to buildings	64–75	Violent storm
General destruction	75 up	Hurricane

5.

There's Water in the Air

Where does the rain come from?

This used to be a great puzzle to the world. Some of the ancient peoples explained rain by saying that there were waters up above the sky. How were the waters held up? Well, the arch of heaven was supposed to hold them up. They thought the rain came down through windows in the firmament, or arch of heaven. When the windows were opened, the rain came down.

They saw the rain fall and run into brooks. They saw

the brooks empty into the rivers and the rivers into the oceans. But they didn't see what fed the clouds. It seemed that after a while all the water would be in the rivers and oceans and there would be no more rain. The ancient Egyptians seldom had rain in their country, but they were glad to depend on the water in the Nile River. They said that people who depended on rain would some day suffer a great calamity.

What they didn't understand is that water evaporates and goes up into the sky. We say that water dries up. And when it does, it turns into an invisible gas and is carried up and away with the winds. And because it is invisible, people could not understand what was going on.

When we talked about the gases that make up the atmosphere we didn't say anything about water vapor. But there is water vapor in the lower atmosphere—or troposphere as the weatherman calls it. Sometimes as much as 5 percent of the total volume of air is water vapor in the form of gas. Generally there is much, much less. We speak of the amount of water vapor in the air as *humidity*.

It is easy to see, now that we have the secret, how the water gets up into the sky. Everybody has seen water vapor being made. The teakettle boils, steam escapes from the spout and makes a little cloud in the kitchen. The cloud starts up toward the ceiling and all of a sudden disappears. The steam has turned into an invisible gas. It has become water vapor.

But you don't need to heat water over a fire in order to turn the water into gas. Water keeps turning into gas all the time even without the aid of a fire. If we set out a pan of water and leave it awhile, the water slowly dries up. If we hang wet clothes on a line, they become dry. In all such cases water has gone up into the atmosphere as a gas.

We call this change *evaporation*. Evaporation takes place from all damp surfaces. Water evaporates from the soil, it evaporates from plants, it evaporates from our bodies. From rivers and lakes and seas and oceans the invisible gas of water is always going up into the atmosphere. The larger the surface, the more evaporation takes place. A good breeze also helps by carrying the moist air away and bringing dry air in its place.

After a while when air is cooled enough, some of the vapor comes out again in a visible form or, as we say, it *condenses*. We see it in such things as mist, fog, cloud, dew, frost, rain, snow and hail. For water is the great

Water goes from the wet clothes into the air as water vapor.

wonder of Nature. It is the only substance that occurs naturally in all the forms of matter—as a solid, as a liquid and as a gas.

The amount of water vapor in the air doesn't stay the same. It is always changing. It comes in at the bottom of the atmosphere by evaporation, mostly from the oceans because there is so much of them. The winds carry it far away. Sooner or later, as it goes up to cooler layers of the atmosphere, it falls out as rain or snow. Very little gets up to the stratosphere. Nearly all the water vapor is in the clouds and stormy weather in the lower part of the atmosphere.

Long after scientists understood about the circulation of water—that is, how it evaporates, condenses, comes

43

down as rain or snow, fills the rivers and oceans and starts evaporating again—they still couldn't understand clouds. What made them float in the air? They knew that the air in clouds is colder than the air around them. "Cold air should be heavier than warm air," they thought. "The many drops of water in clouds should also add to their weight. Why, then, don't they fall to the ground as soon as they are formed?"

The scientists couldn't explain it. As short a time as a century and a half ago they tried to account for clouds staying up in the air by imagining that water drops were bubbles filled with some light gas like hydrogen which lifted them above the earth. At that time the causes of rain and storms were just as great a puzzle to them as the clouds. To find the answers scientists had to learn a good deal about water vapor in the air.

Well, what have they learned?

One thing they have found out is that the atmosphere will not hold an indefinite amount of water vapor. It will hold so much and no more. A great deal of water vapor can be present in the atmosphere and yet it will be quite clear. But there comes a point when no more water vapor can be added. That point is called the *saturation point* or the *dew point*.

The curious thing about the saturation point is that it keeps changing. The amount of water vapor the atmosphere will hold differs under different conditions. It all depends on the temperature. If the temperature rises, more water vapor can be added. If, for example, the temperature is 40° and the air saturated, we can warm the air to 60° and it will be only half saturated. Under such conditions we say the humidity is 50 percent.

But what happens if the air is saturated and instead of raising the temperature we lower it?

Then some of the water vapor will change back from a gas to a liquid. Or, as we say, it will condense. It will come out in fog or cloud.

Let us say the temperature is 60° and the air saturated. We cool it to 40°. Half the water vapor must come out in fog or cloud. If the temperature is 40° and the air saturated and we cool it to 20°, half the water vapor must come out of the air. But this time it won't come out as fog or cloud. The temperature 20° is well below freezing (32°). So the vapor is likely to come out in the form of snow crystals.

That's what happens when we open the door of a refrigerator. The warm air comes in and touches the cold coils and ice pans. It is cooled below the saturation point, and snow crystals collect on the coils and pans. If we set out a glass of ice water in a warm room, the glass "sweats" on the outside. This water doesn't come from inside the glass. It comes from the air. On touching the cold glass, the air is cooled below the saturation point, and the water vapor comes out of the air in droplets of water on the glass.

The same thing happens in Nature. When it does, we call it dew. People say the dew "falls." Actually it doesn't. Dew is formed right where we find it. At night the grass cools off rapidly. The air close to the ground touches the grass and cools off rapidly, too. It cools below the saturation point so the water vapor condenses into droplets on low objects—on grass and flowers and bushes and cobwebs. If the temperature is below freezing, the water vapor comes out in the form of ice crystals. This is frost.

Now what are clouds?

Clouds are condensed water vapor. They are made up of tiny droplets of water or tiny crystals of ice. The particles are so small that a thousand of them set in a row might measure an inch. They are so tiny that the least upward movement of the air holds them up. They are held up by air currents. In many cases air is moving through the clouds from bottom to top all the time.

It is easy to make a cloud. All you have to do is breathe out on a very cold day. A little cloud will form. Or start the kettle steaming, and a little cloud will appear. Believe it or not, all of us have been inside a cloud, for fog is a cloud close to the ground. When we go into a cloud on a mountain, it is just like a fog.

Fogs generally form near a large body of water. They occur when the water is warmer than the land. The moist air moves inland. As it passes over the cold land, the air is cooled. Some of the moisture in it condenses and forms a fog.

But the white, fleecy clouds we see in the sky on a summer day are formed differently. They start out as moist air that is being pushed upward. As the air is

Fog is really a cloud hovering close to the ground.

pushed up, it expands because up there less air is pressing against it. And as it expands, it cools. If it cools enough, the saturation point is reached and some of the water vapor condenses. The result is a cloud. Sometimes the water droplets in it are too small to fall as rain. Unless the water droplets in a cloud join together and increase in size, rain won't fall.

Cloud forms are endless in their variety. Who has not watched the clouds and seen human faces and animal heads, mountains and islands, birds and monstrous fish? No two clouds are alike, and all of them are constantly changing their shape. They are as different as trees are from one another. And yet just as we can say, "This tree is an oak, or a palm tree, or a pine," so we can divide clouds into classes.

About a hundred and fifty years ago an Englishman, Luke Howard by name, thought it would be a good idea to classify the clouds. He divided them into three kinds and gave them Latin names according to what they look like to a person seeing them from the ground. The very high clouds that look like thin streaks or curls he named *cirrus*. The fluffy, white, heaped-up clouds he called *cumulus*. And the gray clouds that make an even layer he named *stratus*. Since then scientists have subdivided clouds into ten classes. All over the world weathermen have agreed to call the different kinds of clouds by these names.

Cirrus clouds are very high, usually four miles or more above the earth. Up there they are in very cold air, and so it is not surprising that they should be made up of ice crystals. High, thin, and white in the sunlight, without shadows, cirrus clouds are sometimes called "mares' tails." Often they are seen far ahead of storms and weather changes.

Cumulus clouds are much lower. They are apt to appear in the late morning or early afternoon of a sunny day. At first they are like balls of cotton with flat bottoms. As the day advances, they become bigger, pushing higher into the atmosphere with swellings like cauliflower. The tops sometimes extend two or three miles above the bases. And the bases are always flat and dark. These bases mark the height where the air becomes saturated. The clouds build up and build up, and finally the sky is nearly filled with them. We can look up between them and see their tops bright in the sunlight, still swelling and pushing upward. Now and then a few drops of rain fall.

Cumulus clouds often are "fair-weather clouds."

Here are ten kinds of clouds named for their form and height.

Miles

5

4

3

2

1

Cirrus

Cirrocumulus

Anvil

Altocumulus

Cumulonimbus

Stratus

Rain

Fog

Not all of these would appear in the sky at the same time.

51

Sometimes, however, they turn into storm clouds. As the cumulus reaches to great heights (three or four miles) and rain begins, we hear thunder and now and then see a flash of lightning. If the cloud is at a distance at this stage, we can see a top shaped like an anvil. The huge upward bulges have reached the freezing level in the high atmosphere. From the great dark base heavy rain falls, sometimes mixed with hail.

Stratus is a low cloud. It is a gray sheet almost without any form. Actually it is a sort of high fog. Often stratus clouds make an even gray layer over the whole sky.

We said a little while ago that clouds are made up of water droplets or ice crystals. But that isn't quite the whole story. Dust is one very important element in the make-up of clouds—and of fogs, too, for a fog is just a stratus cloud on the ground. A drop in the temperature might not by itself cause the moist, pushed-up air to condense. There has to be something for the tiny water droplets or ice crystals to gather on.

Fortunately the air has plenty of minute dust particles. They are like the tiny specks we see in a sunbeam—particles of soil, soot from factory chimneys, smoke of fires. Some of the "dust" is grains of pollen, bacteria, seeds, and salt from ocean spray. Of this kind of dust more is present, naturally, in the lower atmosphere, but some is carried to heights of several miles. The dust of burning meteors and volcanic explosions furnishes a supply of dust particles for the very high atmosphere. Most of these particles are so small we cannot see them.

In cities there is, of course, more dust than in the country. In a smoky city there may be as many as 100,000 dust particles per cubic centimeter, which is a space about the size of a small marble. Water droplets in a fog mixed with the smoke may become very dense over a city. The mixture is called *smog*.

At certain times, also, there is more dust than at other times. When in the year 1883 the volcanic island Krakatoa off southeast Asia blew up, the ashes shot up to a height of 17 miles, and a black pall of dust stretched out for 150 miles. Thin, brownish clouds of Krakatoa dust were carried by the winds over the whole earth for several months afterward.

6.

Rain, Snow, Hail, Sleet

Rain is so important that scientists are anxious to learn more about it. There are two big questions they have tried to answer. First, why doesn't it rain sometimes when everything seems to be right? Second, why can't we help Nature a little and bring on rain when we need it?

For centuries men have been trying to help Nature make rain. In ancient times some people thought the frog was the god of waters. So when there was no rain, they beat frogs with sticks to make them bring on the rain. Now and then it did rain a little. That kept the poor frogs in trouble, for people thought the beating caused the rain.

In some tribes men would cover themselves with down from birds to make them look like clouds. Then they would dance around hoping that Nature would follow their example and make clouds. If there were clouds, rain might follow. If the dancers made a noise like thunder, they thought Nature would make thunder, too. If people threw a little water on one another, they thought Nature would pour a lot of water on them.

The curious thing is that such rainmakers very often succeed in "bringing" rain. They are very clever. In the first place, they never try to make it rain in regions where rain never falls. Nor do they try to make it at periods other than when rain usually comes. Also they never try to make rain until rain is long overdue. And usually they are careful to engage in ceremonies that will take up a lot of time. By the time they have finished with their dances and their hocus-pocus, the long overdue rain often arrives—and the rainmakers get the credit for having brought it.

Modern scientific rainmaking is a different sort of

thing. We understand a little about the laws of rain now, and our efforts to make it come down are not based on magic. We don't try to make Nature do the impossible. We try to create the conditions it needs.

Scientists use the word *precipitation* to mean rain, snow, hail, and other things that come from water vapor in the atmosphere. They say that in the high tops of clouds there are usually ice crystals which bring precipitation. Also there are extremely small water droplets. The ice crystals gather the water droplets and grow in size. They begin to fall and gather more water droplets. Whether snow or rain falls depends on the temperatures in the top of the cloud and in the air between the cloud and the earth. If the temperatures are mostly below freezing, snow will fall. If not, the ice crystals will melt into raindrops.

It is on the basis of this theory that the modern scientific rainmakers work. Sometimes they go up in an airplane and scatter dry ice pellets or other chemicals into the clouds. More often they send chemicals up in the form of smoke. Or, as they say, they "seed" the clouds with chemicals. By doing that they hope to increase precipitation. They hope to bring more of the cloud droplets to earth.

Rainmakers sometimes scatter dry ice pellets on the clouds.

But nobody who has to do with modern rainmaking really believes man will ever be able to produce large amounts of rain over any large area. The forces of Nature which take part in making the world's rain are so tremendous that it is beyond our power to duplicate them. To cover a square mile with one inch of rain takes 72,300 tons of water. To cover an average state with one inch of rain takes 3 or 4 billions of tons. Every second, it has been estimated, 16 million tons of rain, hail, and snow fall on the face of the earth. And all of this enormous quantity of water first has to be evaporated and lifted high into the air.

Even if all the water vapor in all of the air above us at any one time suddenly condensed, it would make a layer of water only an inch deep. This means that Nature must bring a lot more moist air over us fast to make a really big rain.

Rain, Snow, Hail, Sleet

What do we mean by a big rain?

First, let's see what ordinary rain amounts to. In the average year, San Francisco gets a little more than 20 inches of precipitation (rain and melted snow). Chicago has more than 30, New York City more than 40. Usually more rain falls in warmer regions where there is more moisture in the air. New Orleans has more than 50 inches in a year.

In the world's biggest rains, more than 20 inches have fallen in Texas in three hours—a year's rain at San Francisco. More than 30 inches have fallen in five hours in Pennsylvania. More than 80 inches in three days in Jamaica. The wettest spot in the world is in India at a place named Cherrapunji. At this place 100 inches have fallen in four days, 366 inches in one month and more than 1,000 inches in one year.

What causes these huge amounts of rain at Cherrapunji? Hot, very moist winds come rapidly from the Indian Ocean and blow up a steep mountain slope. The air expands and cools quickly. It goes far below the saturation point, and heavy rain comes down. As fast as the air drops its moisture, it moves on. More hot, moist air takes its place, and the heavy rain continues. These winds are a part of the great Asiatic monsoon. They blow all during the warm season, from the ocean toward the interior of Asia. In midsummer the *average* rainfall is more than 100 inches a month.

In December and January the wind blows the opposite direction at Cherrapunji. It is pretty dry—much less than one inch in a month.

Snow is not, as some people say, frozen rain. Snow has never been water. It is water vapor that has turned directly into ice crystals.

When seen under a microscope, the little crystals of snow are very lacy and beautiful and varied. Seldom, if ever, are two of them exactly alike. Yet all are six-sided or six-pointed. A tiny snowflake may be made of a single crystal. Large flakes are made up of many crystals. Like raindrops, each one is formed around a tiny dust or other particle.

Sometimes snowflakes are very large. The biggest known fell in Montana in 1887 at a place named Fort Keogh. Some of them fell on a bare field near the Fort and made great white splotches. They were 15 inches across and 8 inches thick! Single snowflakes that would fill a teacup have fallen at other places.

On the other hand, in extremely cold weather—as in a blizzard in the Dakotas and Nebraska—snow is fine

Snow and ice on a mountainside may cause an avalanche.

and powdery. It is blown by high winds. The air is so full of it that people and animals get it in their lungs and suffocate.

Even though snow is very light in weight, it piles up in mountain districts and causes avalanches. Once started, an avalanche gathers tremendous power. Trees are snapped off at the ground, and buildings are carried away. Millions of dollars are spent in building barriers to keep avalanches from destroying towns, highways and railroads.

In the United States the biggest snows are in California on the west slopes of the Sierra Nevada Mountains. Here the moist winds come up the slope from the Pacific Ocean. In a single day 60 inches fell at a place named Giant Forest. During the winter of 1906–07 the snowfall at Tamarack, California, totaled 884 inches, more than 73 feet!

Snow is not frozen rain, but hail and sleet are. Yet hail and sleet are formed differently. Hailstones are great adventurers. As a rule the larger they are the more adventures they have been through.

Hailstones vary greatly in size. It is not unusual to find them as large as mothballs, but sometimes they are as large as baseballs or larger. The largest hailstones on record came down in July, 1928, at Potter, Nebraska, and measured seventeen inches around. One of them weighed one and a half pounds! Many were as large as grapefruit. It is easy to see that big hailstones like this can do a great deal of harm to crops and break much glass in hothouses. It has been figured out that in still air a hailstone an inch and a half through the middle would fall at a speed of 60 miles an hour. A hailstone five inches through the middle would fall at 120 miles an hour. No wonder that during one severe storm in India the hail killed buffaloes!

In the central part of the United States the losses to farmers from hail amount to millions of dollars every year. Sometimes a crop is completely destroyed by a single storm. A heavy fall of hail has been known to strip all the leaves from plants and trees.

What makes these balls of ice and snow? How do they get to be as big as baseballs and bigger?

Hailstones are born of the thundercloud. If we cut

The largest hailstones on record measured 17 inches around.

a hailstone through the middle, we see that it is made up of layers like an onion, only the layers are ice and snow, ice and snow. Those layers tell us how hailstones are made.

After the raindrops are formed, up-draughts inside the thundercloud lift them up into the freezing zone where snow is forming in the cloud. The raindrops turn to ice. At the same time they get a coating of snow. Now they are much heavier than they were as raindrops, and if the up-draught of air in the cloud weakens, they start to fall. As they get into the rain levels of the cloud, they bump into raindrops and get a coating of rain. Then again an up-draught comes and lifts them to freezing heights. The water coating turns to ice, and the hailstones get another covering of snow before they fall. Sometimes they are carried up many times. Such hailstones will grow very large. But in the end all become too heavy for the air to support them. Large or small, finally the hailstones fall to the ground.

As for sleet, it is just frozen rain to which no adventures have happened. It is rain that freezes into clear beads of ice because it passes through a layer of cold air before reaching the ground. The beads bounce when they strike the earth.

Rain, Snow, Hail, Sleet

Rain that freezes immediately *after* falling is called glaze. The storm which causes it is called an ice storm. Glaze causes great damage to trees and electric wires because the weight of ice is so great, especially when a thick coating is formed. Oftentimes a deposit of glaze is as much as two inches thick. When that happens, great branches break under the weight and wires are pulled down.

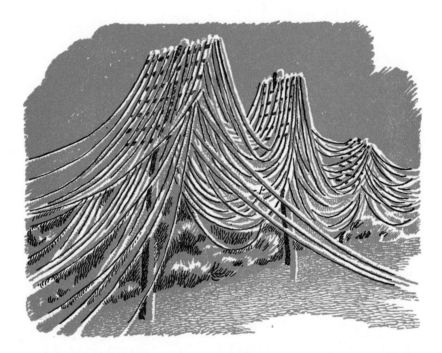

In an ice storm, glaze causes great damage to trees and wires.

7.

Storms—Good and Bad

Of all the scenes in the drama of weather, storms are the most exciting. And of all storms, the one we see most often is the thunderstorm. Every single day of the year the world has 44,000 of them. In polar regions they aren't to be seen very often, but in the tropics they are extremely common. Down in Panama and over in Java the average is 200 thunderstorm days a year. Right now at this moment 1,800 thunderstorms are raging over the earth.

What makes them? How are they born?

Storms—Good and Bad

Thunderstorms occur when there is a great difference in the temperature between the air close to the earth and the air up high. That might happen because the air near the earth has been heated or the air up above has been greatly cooled. Most of the ocean thunderstorms are caused by cooling up above. In our part of the world, however, a thunderstorm more often occurs because the sun has heated the ground and the air above it has become very warm. They are caused also by cold air pushing under warm moist air and lifting it. Also by moist winds blowing up the side of a mountain.

With us a thunderstorm is very apt to start on a quiet summer afternoon when there is lots of moisture in the air. The overheated surface air is pushed up by cooler air around it. Pretty soon a fluffy white cumulus cloud forms. It grows and grows, piles up very deep, three miles deep perhaps, and starts getting darker and darker. The threatening cloud moves eastward. Suddenly lightning begins to flash, thunder to roll. Strong gusts of cold wind come straight from the storm. Small trees bend before them, dead branches break from the great trees. Then slowly the wind dies, and rain comes down in bucketfuls. Sometimes hail comes with it. Flash after flash lights up the sky. The thunder rolls. Heavy rain may last only a few minutes. Certainly in an hour or two everything is over. The sky clears. Gentle winds blow again from the south. And peace is restored.

Most thunderstorms are local storms. Generally they are only a few miles wide. But sometimes a line of

The cloud of a thunderstorm may pile up three miles deep.

thunderstorms extends for 100 miles or more. It may travel for hundreds of miles.

Often the path of a thunderstorm is very clearly marked. Within that path the rain may come down very heavily. Yet a short distance away not a drop will fall.

Of course, the most impressive part of a thunderstorm is the lightning and thunder. Time was when people were terrified by them. The Greeks thought angry Zeus, king of the gods, was hurling thunderbolts forged for him by the lame smith Vulcan. Nowadays everybody knows that lightning is just a huge electric spark. Everybody knows that thunder is just a noise. It is the sound made by rapidly expanding air when lightning passes through it and heats it. The lightning is extremely hot—perhaps 1,500° C. After it tears the atmosphere apart, the air comes together with a bang.

What causes these huge electric sparks which make savages fall on their knees in terror?

The sparks occur because the droplets of water in the cloud and also the air around them become charged with electricity. The same thing happens to the snow crystals in the top part of the cloud. They, too, become charged with electricity. Tension is built up. And finally there is too much. A discharge of electricity takes place. Sometimes it takes place within the cloud, sometimes between one cloud and another, sometimes between the cloud and the earth.

In a single storm there may be several thousand flashes. When the discharge is between cloud and earth, the path may be a mile long. Between cloud and cloud it may be much longer. The branching of the lightning flashes is very clear to see if the storm is near. It may take a whole second sometimes before a flash is finished. Generally, however, it is over much sooner. At times the path of the lightning cannot be seen at all. That happens when a storm is far off. The cloud and the sky merely light up suddenly in what we call "sheet lightning."

As for the thunder, sometimes it rumbles and sometimes it claps. Sometimes it sounds like an artillery battle. The rumbling is the echoing of the thunder in the clouds. When there is a flash and sudden clap, you may be sure the storm is right overhead. The lightning and thunder never come at the same instant, of course, because light travels almost a million times faster than sound and reaches us sooner. You can tell how far away the thunderstorm is by counting the seconds between the flash of lightning and the crash of thunder. Sound travels a mile in five seconds. So if it takes fifteen seconds between lightning and thunder, the storm is three miles away.

Thunderstorms are so common in some parts of our country that on a sultry day many people look forward to one with pleasure rather than fear. "It will cool things off," they say. Also these storms often bring rain when it is badly needed. But in our Great Plains and Mississippi Valley, people don't always look for a thunderstorm with pleasure. For there the thunder and lightning and rain may come with something else—the dread tornado. Though just a little storm, the tornado is of all storms on earth the most violent.

The tornado comes up suddenly like any thunderstorm. People see a thick, dark cloud approaching from the distance. As it comes nearer, they see a funnel-shaped piece of the cloud dangling down. It looks like a huge elephant's trunk. The trunk or funnel whips around in different directions. It rises and falls. Where the funnel touches the ground, it picks up nearly everything in its path and makes a terrible noise.

When people see such a sight, they think of just one thing—safety. If the funnel is moving to the right or the left of them, it is likely that the tornado will pass them by. If it seems to stand still, it may be coming either straight toward them or straight away. They don't stop to find out which. In Kansas and other states where tornadoes are most frequent many people have a "cyclone cellar" some distance from their farm buildings.

Where tornadoes are frequent, people hide in cyclone cellars.

Into this they clamber and stay put till the storm passes. It doesn't take long. The tornado travels at 20 to 40 miles an hour; so at any one spot everything is over in about half a minute. But in that half minute terrible destruction takes place. The tornado can level everything it touches except the best steel-braced buildings.

Often the tornado is called a "twister," and for a very

good reason—its winds are whirling winds. With a deafening roar and at a terrific speed—200, 300, perhaps even 500 miles an hour—they race around the low pressure at the center of the tornado. At the same time there is an up-draught in the center that lifts the air at 100 or 200 miles an hour.

Everything the funnel touches is doomed. Not only does the wind level nearly anything that stands up in its path. Inside the funnel the air pressure is so low that houses and barns and silos simply "explode" as the funnel passes over them. The same thing happens as with a balloon that is blown up too much. The pressure inside the building being greater than the pressure inside the tornado, the walls and roofs blow out. At the same time the up-draught in the center picks up even heavy objects like automobiles and cattle and horses and people and carries them away—sometimes long distances. And it may set them down again quite unharmed.

But why should tornadoes be frequent in the central part of our country and not elsewhere?

The answer is that just here two very different air currents meet. Moist and warm, one current comes in from the Gulf of Mexico. A current of dry, cold air blows across the top of the moist current. The contrast

In a tornado, buildings may explode as the funnel passes over.

between the two air currents supplies the energy. Something starts the upward motion; we are not sure what. The warm air is swept upward and a whirling motion starts up at the level of the cloud. Once started, the winds keep whirling around more and more madly.

Luckily the path of a tornado is only 1,000 feet wide on the average and rarely more than 25 miles long. So the destruction is not widespread. A tropical cyclone does much more damage. For though it blows with less fury than the tornado, it is a much bigger storm. It may cover many thousands of square miles. And instead of lasting a half minute, it may take 24 hours to pass.

A tropical cyclone is like a tornado in that it is a whirling storm. The word "cyclone" shows that. It means "coil of a snake." In different parts of the world different names are applied to this dreaded storm. It is called typhoon, cyclone, willy-willy, baguio. In our part of the world we know it as the hurricane.

All along our Gulf Coast and Eastern Seaboard as far north as New England people are "hurricane conscious." But it is around the Gulf of Mexico and the West Indies that the hurricane is feared most. For in times past whole cities have been wiped out and thousands of lives lost in a single storm. No other report of the Weather

Bureau is watched for more anxiously than the warning that a hurricane is on its way.

Like all tropical cyclones the whirling winds of a hurricane are born over the ocean near the equator. The winds circle around a center the way they do in a tornado. But there is a difference. In the center of the tornado there is a terrific up-draught that can pick up an automobile and carry it off. In the center of a hurricane there is a calm. Sometimes this calm is absolute. And yet right close to the center the winds blow with the greatest fury. Their speed is sometimes 150 miles an hour and more. At times a gust will blow at 250 miles an hour.

Many mariners have described the fury of the hurricane as it passed over their ship and the strange lull in the center of the storm. Sometimes the lull lasts for three hours or more. While a ship is passing through the calm center or "eye" of the storm, the roar of the hurricane winds on all sides may be distinctly heard. The weather partly clears. By day the sun shines through and the banks of hurricane clouds may be seen at the horizon. By night the stars come out.

Fortunately hurricanes don't often travel inland. When they do, the damage to property is terrific.

Storms—Good and Bad

Buildings are wrecked, whole forests are uprooted. Yet, strangely, the greatest loss of life in a hurricane is not due directly to the wind. Three quarters of the casualties are due to the great waves driven like a wall of water by storm winds over low coastal areas. The storm waves sometimes come so suddenly that people can't escape from them. One hurricane wave that struck a Cuban town in 1932 drowned 2,500 persons. Another, in the Bay of Bengal, took 20,000 lives. A third, in the same region, took a toll of 300,000.

There is no storm that makes a person feel quite so small and powerless as a hurricane, and anyone who has ever been through a bad one will never forget it. Man plans to conquer space. But he doesn't have much hope of taming the hurricane. The forces that take part in a hurricane are so gigantic that man scarcely dreams of controlling them. Such weather seems beyond man's power now or ever. All man can do now is observe, report, predict, and warn.

8.

How We Measure and Observe the Weather

Observe, report, predict, and warn—these are the things weathermen try to do. And now that we have talked about the atmosphere and discussed the different acts it puts on, let us see how weathermen work.

First, let us make a visit to a place where people are observing and measuring the weather.

What do they want to find out? Everything possible, of course. And everything possible adds up to a good deal. We will list the principal items.

How We Measure and Observe the Weather

1. Air pressure
2. Direction of the wind
3. Velocity of the wind
4. Temperature of the air
5. Humidity
6. Amount, kind, and height of clouds
7. Amount of rain or snow
8. Visibility

All together these elements make up what we call weather. Let us get acquainted with some of the instruments the weathermen use to observe and measure it.

Several of the older instruments catch our eye even before we enter the weather office. They stand outside, high up on top of the building. They are the wind instruments. Near by we see a rain gauge and a shelter for thermometers.

We will start with the rain gauge, for no doubt it is the oldest weather instrument in the world. Very early in his career, man the farmer needed to know about rainfall, and he quickly found out how he could measure it. He learned that any open vessel set outdoors would serve as a crude rain gauge. And what he discovered serves us still. Only we have worked out some new ideas.

How We Measure and Observe the Weather

Any straight-sided vessel placed at a distance from trees and other objects that might interfere with the rainfall does pretty well. There is just one trouble. On level ground rain doesn't show much. Even a heavy rain measures only an inch or two. For this reason, a measure even in tenths of an inch is too coarse. We have to be able to measure rain in hundredths of an inch, for even that small amount is important. Even that small amount of rainfall makes more than a ton of water per acre.

So what do we do?

We catch the rain in a big can, and then empty the water into another can or tube with a bottom one-tenth as big. There is our rain ten times as deep as it was in the big can. Now it is easy to measure the rainfall to the hundredth part of an inch.

Weathermen use this tipping bucket gauge to measure rainfall.

Of course, that doesn't tell us *when* the rain fell. A clever device is needed for that, and you may be sure there is one. It is called the tipping bucket. The tipping bucket is a small, flat bucket divided in the middle. It is balanced on a frame and set under a cone-shaped rain spout. When one-hundredth of an inch of rain has come down the spout and run into one side of the bucket, it tips. That much water weighs just enough to tip the bucket and dump the rain into the gauge below. As it tips, the empty side of the bucket comes under the spout all ready to catch the next hundredth of an inch of rain. When the second side of the bucket goes down and dumps, the first side comes under the spout again. The rain itself does all the work.

But this isn't quite all. Electrical wires run from the tipping bucket to a register in the office. Every time the bucket tips, a pen in the office makes a mark on a register sheet. So we know exactly when the bucket tipped each time.

As for snow, we measure it in two ways. One way is to push a stick into the snow on level ground in three places. Then the average of the three is used as the depth of snowfall (unmelted). The other way is to melt the snow collected in the gauge and measure the water.

Usually the melting is done by mixing a certain amount of warm water with the snow. Then the melted mixture is measured, and the amount of warm water is subtracted. Ordinarily, when we melt the snow caught in the gauge, the depth of water we get is about one-tenth the depth of the snow.

Now for the wind instruments. One of them is almost as old as the rain gauge and so common that everyone knows it. It is the wind vane. It tells the direction of the wind. Oftentimes people call it the weather vane because the direction from which the wind blows is a good indication of the coming weather. In former days it was customary to make the wind vane in the shape of a rooster. The modern wind vane generally has an arrow for a head and a wide tail to catch the wind. The arrow points *into* the wind; that is, it points in the direction the wind is coming from. The weatherman's wind vane is connected by wires into the weather office, where it registers the direction of the wind on a sheet of paper wound around a drum turned by clockwork.

On a short arm just below the wind vane on top of the building is another wind instrument. It is a whirling gauge called an *anemometer*. It measures the speed, or velocity, of wind.

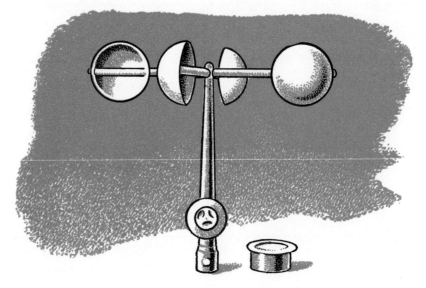

This four-cup anemometer measures the speed of the wind.

In the United States the most common anemometer has four cups which catch the wind and are turned by it. The stronger the wind, the faster the cups turn. Most anemometers are wired to a register in the weather office. As the cups turn, the miles are marked on a cylinder driven by clockwork. Some anemometers are connected by wires to an electric buzzer. The observer can press a button and listen. The number of buzzes he hears per minute tells him the number of miles per hour the wind is blowing.

The last of the instruments standing outside—but in a special shelter to protect them from sun and rain and snow—are the thermometers. A thermometer, as you know, measures heat. A doctor's thermometer measures the heat of the body, but a weatherman's thermometer measures the heat, or the temperature, of the air. In the bulb of the thermometer there is a quantity of mercury. As the bulb is warmed, the mercury in it expands and goes up a narrow bore in the glass. The more the mercury is heated, the higher it rises in the tube.

In the shelter there are quite a few thermometers. One keeps a continuous record of the temperature. It is called a *thermograph* because it makes a graph, or picture, of the temperature changes. This thermometer is quite special. It usually has a curved metal tube instead of glass and contains alcohol. As the temperature changes, the shape of the tube changes. A recording pen is fastened to one end of the tube. The pen moves as the tube changes shape and makes a mark on a sheet of paper wrapped around a drum. There is clockwork inside it that keeps the paper turning. The sheet of paper is ruled in hours. So the weatherman can tell just what the temperature was at any time during the day or night. Most thermographs will keep a record for a

The pen of the thermograph records temperature changes.

whole week before the sheet has to be changed.

Of course, people always want to know what was the highest temperature in the day and what was the lowest. So in the shelter there are two thermometers that record just that. One thermometer goes up and stays at the highest point reached during the day. It works like a doctor's thermometer. Right above the bulb there is a narrow place in the glass tube. As the temperature of the air rises, the mercury expands and is forced through the narrow place. When the air gets cooler, the mercury stands still. It can't get down past the narrow place. To get it back into the bulb, the thermometer has to be whirled or shaken.

The other thermometer goes down and stays down at the lowest temperature reached. This thermometer has alcohol in it instead of mercury because alcohol, while it expands and contracts like mercury, freezes at a lower temperature. It can therefore work even when it is very cold. In the glass tube of this alcohol thermometer there is a little piece of glass, called an *index*. The index floats in the alcohol. As the temperature falls, the film at the upper end of the alcohol column draws the index down toward the bulb. When the temperature rises, the alcohol flows up again past the index. But the thermometer is hung on its side, and the index stays down at the low point. Because this thermometer shows the lowest temperature reached, it is called the *minimum thermometer*. The other is called the *maximum thermometer*. In the weather office they are often referred to as *max* and *min*.

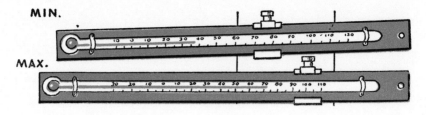

Twin thermometers record highest and lowest temperatures.

In the shelter there is another pair of thermometers. They are the wet-and-dry. The dry thermometer gives the temperature of the air. The wet one is so called because around the bulb it has a bit of muslin which the observer wets before he takes a reading. He wets it and sends a stream of air from a fan onto the wet bulb. As the water on the muslin evaporates, it causes the temperature of the wet thermometer to fall. The drier the air the more evaporation and cooling. The observer reads both thermometers and finds the difference between them. From that figure he can get the humidity and the dew point. He doesn't have to work these out. Everything has been figured out for him. All he has to do is refer to a set of tables, and there is his answer.

The pair of wet-and-dry thermometers is also called a *psychrometer*. The psychrometer is very accurate, but it doesn't give a continuous record. So in the weatherman's thermometer shelter there is often another instrument that does that. It is called a *hygrograph*.

A hygrograph works on a very delicate principle. Perhaps you know that a hair grows longer when there is more moisture in the air and shorter when the air is drier. This is the principle on which the hygrograph is made. Strands of human hair are attached to a pen in

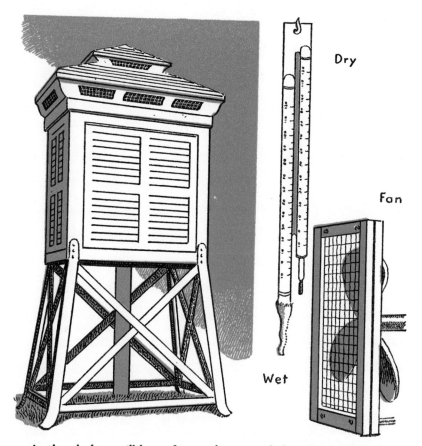

Dry

Fan

Wet

In the shelter will be a fan and wet-and-dry thermometers.

such a way that as the hair changes length, a mark is traced on a moving piece of paper.

But not all the instruments are out of doors. The pressure of the atmosphere can be measured just as well indoors as outside. The observer can step to the *barometer* in his office and find out what the air pressure is.

The barometer is one of the most important instruments a weatherman has. For changes in air pressure play a very important part in the weather. A drop in the air pressure, for example, may well mean that bad weather is on the way. When the air pressure is rising, you can generally expect fair weather.

The barometer isn't nearly as old as the rain gauge or the wind vane. Still, it is one of the older instruments. It goes back about three hundred years, to the time right after the great astronomer Galileo.

Galileo himself was very much interested in the question of the weight of the atmosphere. He was certain that although invisible, air is a substance and has weight. He made an experiment to prove it. He took a tube of air, plugged it up and weighed it. Then he forced more air into it, plugged it up again, and weighed it once more. The tube weighed a little more. But how

Torricelli experimented with a long, glass tube of mercury.

much did the atmosphere weigh? Galileo's experiment didn't show that.

It was one of his pupils, Torricelli by name, who thought up a way of showing just how much the atmosphere weighed. He invented the barometer.

Torricelli took a long, glass tube closed at one end. He filled it with mercury. Then he put his finger over the open end and turned the tube upside down. He held his finger there to keep the mercury from running out. Then, keeping his finger in place, he set the open end in the bowl containing the mercury. When he took his finger away, a little of the mercury ran out of the tube into the mercury in the bowl, but the column of mercury stayed. The column was nearly 30 inches high. Up at the top was a clear space. It wasn't filled with air because no air could get into the tube. The space was just empty—a vacuum.

Why did the mercury stay up that high in the tube? Because the air outside was pressing on the mercury in the bowl. It was pressing hard enough to push the mercury up nearly 30 inches in the tube. With a shorter tube it would push the mercury right up against the top of the tube. But the air can only push hard enough to hold up 29 or 30 inches of mercury which is very heavy.

Torricelli had discovered how to weigh the atmosphere. But soon afterward another exciting discovery was made. People noticed that the column of mercury in the barometer didn't always stay the same height. Sometimes the mercury was high; sometimes it was low. That must mean the air pressure changed.

Of course, it was easy to understand that if you took the barometer up a mountain, the column of mercury would fall. That was because the air pressure on a mountain was less than at sea level. For there is less air above us the higher up we go. But people noticed that even when the barometer stayed in the same place, the mercury sometimes changed its level in the tube. The air pressure, then, was different at different times. And another thing. The air pressure and the weather seemed to change together. When the mercury was high in the tube, the weather was generally good. When the mercury was low, the weather was bad.

That is how the barometer came into use as an instrument to predict the weather. Barometer makers marked the dial of the barometer to indicate what kind of weather was to be expected. The marks said, "Stormy," "Rain," "Change," "Fair," "Very Dry," and so forth. Such indicators are still used today. They help a little to predict the weather. Modern forecasters, as we shall see, use other methods. Still, nearly all weather forecasters will tell you the barometer is the most important instrument they have. Whatever else is lacking in a weather forecasting office, you may be sure the barometer is there.

The mercury barometer is the most accurate instrument for measuring air pressure. But it doesn't keep a record. The weatherman needs a record on a sheet of

When the barometer is high, the weather is generally good.

paper so he can see whether the air pressure has been rising or falling and how fast. That's important in forecasting.

For this he uses a *barograph*. It has a metal box with the air taken out instead of a glass tube with an empty space at the top. The air pushes on the box as it tries to get in. The pressure on the box makes a pen go up or down on a sheet. This works just as well inside the weather office as outside. The air pressure can't be kept out of the office.

It is very handy to have all these dials and registers

in the weather office. Then the weatherman doesn't have to run up on the roof every time he gets a phone call asking for the wind direction or velocity, the temperature or the rainfall.

During a big storm it is exciting to watch the weather instruments in the office. Great gusts of wind roar around the building. Inside you can see how hard it is blowing by watching the rise and fall of the pen on the wind register. The vane outside swings back and forth in powerful air currents and makes a zigzag line on the paper. Heavy rain falls and makes a mark on the sheet for every hundredth part of an inch. On the barograph you see at first a steep fall in air pressure. You know that the storm will keep up or get worse until after the pen begins to go up on the barograph sheet.

The pen of the barograph records changes in air pressure.

9.

What's Happening
in the Upper Air?

So far all the instruments we saw at the weather office are the old ones. They have long been used to measure weather conditions at the surface of the earth. But now we must get acquainted with some of the strange instruments which have recently been put to use by weathermen, mostly to measure conditions in the upper air. Also we want to find out what is measured without any instruments at all.

Out behind the weather office we see a young man putting helium gas into a big rubber balloon. In a few minutes it will rise to explore the atmosphere. Balloons like this go up twice a day or oftener at more than sixty weather offices in the United States. Each one carries a small box and a parachute to lower the box to earth after the balloon bursts high in the air.

This little box is the outcome of the dreams of many people both in and out of the weather bureaus of the world. For as long as fifty years ago scientists realized that we would never do much better in predicting the weather till we knew something of what was happening in the upper levels of the atmosphere. We would have to know the temperature, the pressure, and the humidity up there.

But how were people to find out? Instruments that would record these things were heavy. If they were sent up on balloons, the instruments would have to come down by parachute. The weather forecasters would have to wait till the parachutes landed. After that it would take time to study the records. And by then, the weather would be here.

People tried sending weather instruments up by kites, but kites couldn't get high enough. When the wind was light, they couldn't go up at all. And the kite wires were dangerous to airplanes besides.

Then for a while scientists tried getting instruments up in airplanes. For several years, beginning in the thirties, *meteorographs*, as such instruments are called, were carried up regularly in airplanes. The planes rose to about 15 or 20 thousand feet. But in stormy weather they couldn't go up. And that's just when the records were needed most.

"What we want," the weather forecasters said, "is a meteorograph and a radio transmitter which could be sent up together on a balloon. If such a thing could be devised, then we wouldn't have to wait for the instruments to drop by parachute. The radio would send down signals giving us the weather data from the meteorograph as the balloon was carrying it up."

About twenty years ago such a device was actually made and soon was put into operation. It is called a *radiosonde*. The radiosonde started a new era in weather forecasting.

The young man we see behind the weather office is putting helium in the balloon to use with a radiosonde. The box that will go up into the air is a quite amazing instrument. It weighs less than two pounds. Yet it will measure the temperature, pressure, and humidity of the atmosphere and send back signals all during the balloon's

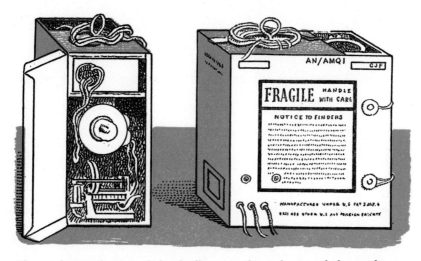

The radiosonde travels by balloon and sends signals by radio.

journey. The signals will be received on a recorder in the weather office. Long before the balloon bursts and the box comes down by parachute, the observer will know what things are like aloft.

Getting the direction and speed of winds up there is also important now that the sky has become a highway. For more than thirty years small balloons—without instruments—have been sent up to get these facts. These *pilot balloons* are sent up four times a day at more than 150 places in the United States.

Usually a pilot balloon contains just enough helium gas to make it go up at the rate of about 600 feet a minute. As the balloon rises, the winds at different levels

97

carry it along. At the end of each minute someone below observes the position of the balloon by means of a sort of surveying instrument, a *theodolite*, and records the direction and speed of the wind at each level.

On sunny days a clear rubber balloon is used. That's because sunlight reflects on the walls of the balloon and makes it visible far away. The balloon looks like a star—just a point of light. On cloudy days red rubber balloons are sent up. They show up plainly against the white background of clouds. At night color doesn't matter. At night a small flashlight is attached to make the balloon visible.

For many years there was no way to measure the speed of winds above the clouds. The pilot balloons would get lost in the clouds, sometimes quite close to the earth. This was serious because in cloudy and stormy weather the information would be missing just when it was needed most.

Then in World War II radar was developed.

Radar is one of the most remarkable things in the world. It is like something right out of a fairy tale. It can find things a hundred miles away. It can find them on the darkest night.

The way it works is this. A powerful radio beam is

The balloon will carry the radiosonde into high altitudes. The observer at the left will follow the flight by radio.

What's Happening in the Upper Air?

Radar (left) and the screen (right) showing the echo.

sent out. When the beam strikes an object, some of the energy is reflected back to the receiver and appears as a milky image on a screen. This reflection is called an echo.

You may be sure it wasn't long before someone thought of using radar to trace balloons in cloudy and stormy weather. All that was needed was to attach a piece of metal to the balloon. Then radar would follow it long after the balloon passed into the clouds.

By means of radar it is now possible to record the speed of winds above the clouds. At many places in the United States radar is put to work to track balloons.

Radar is amazing. It can find the most unbelievable things. During the war it was found that radar echoes came from places where rain was falling. So now the weathermen put radar to work to detect thunderstorms that are too far away to be visible to the eye.

Other kinds of instruments are used, too. Airplane pilots need very special information. It is not surprising, therefore, that in a weather office at an airport very special instruments are to be found. There is the *ceilometer*, for example.

When landing in cloudy weather, a pilot needs to know the height of the cloud base, his *ceiling*, so-called. For he must know how high above the ground he will be when he breaks out of the clouds and can see the runway. The ceilometer, which measures the ceiling for

An airplane pilot gets cloud ceilings measured by a ceilometer.

him, is really three instruments in one. The first is a projector. That sends a beam of light up against the bottom of the cloud. The second is a detector. Placed about 1,000 feet from the projector, the detector's job is to scan the spotlight on the clouds and register the angle at which the spot is seen. From this angle the height of the cloud base is figured. The job of the third part of the ceilometer is to keep a record of the observations.

In places where a ceilometer is not a part of the equipment, other devices are used to measure the height of the cloud ceiling. One of the simplest is the ceiling balloon. It is a little red, purple or white rubber balloon filled with hydrogen or helium. The weatherman knows the exact rate at which the balloon rises. So he can measure the height of the ceiling by the length of time the balloon takes to reach the clouds.

Another thing very important to airplane pilots coming in for a landing is *visibility*—the distance, that is, at which an object is just barely visible to the naked eye. If a pilot knows the visibility at a place where he is going to land, he knows how far ahead he can see the runway. This is important, for the plane moves very fast. At night visibility is the distance at which lights can be seen. As yet there is no instrument that will measure visibility day or night. The observer has to make his observations with his own eyes.

The kind of clouds that are in the sky and the total amount of cloudiness are also facts which the observer must determine for himself. Fortunately, although there are ten classes of clouds, weathermen are so familiar with them that they have no difficulty in identifying them. And as for the total amount of clouds in the sky, that becomes a less difficult problem when the observer makes his estimate in tenths of the sky covered. If the sky is entirely covered, he records it as 10. If there are no clouds at all, he records it as 0. If half covered, 5, etc.

Along with other facts the observer's reports of clouds are telegraphed far and wide and sent around the world by radio. For clouds are the skywriting of the weather. Every cloud has a message, and few big changes in the weather are not heralded by Nature's writing in the sky.

10.

Predicting the Weather

Our weather of tomorrow is a long way off today. It moves along at maybe 30 miles an hour—not as fast as a heavy truck on the highway. But unlike the truck, the weather makes no stops. So at the end of 24 hours it has moved 720 miles!

It is for this reason—because weather moves—that the best way to predict it is by the use of a map. A map gives a picture of the weather over a broad area. And we need a broad picture. For storms and other conditions which cause weather changes are spread out over vast regions. Our winter storms of rain and snow are often 1,000 miles across. How much of such a storm could we see with our own eyes? Even from a high place on a mountain we could see only a very small part. Even with all our instruments in only one place we could know very little about it.

Scientists for centuries tried to predict the weather from what one man could see. We can understand now why they didn't have much success. They didn't appreciate the fact that weather moves. In our country the fact that storms travel seemed a very startling notion even at the time when Benjamin Franklin suggested it. In Europe the idea was held by several scientists. But it wasn't easy to prove. Finally a German professor by the name of Heinrich Brandes made a study of French weather reports. Then he wrote a paper to prove that weather doesn't stand still and that its movements could be traced on a map. He convinced the scientists that if reports could be collected quickly enough and maps drawn, the movement of storms and some other weather changes could be predicted.

But that was in 1820. There was no telegraph then. Collecting reports quickly enough was just a dream.

Predicting the Weather

It is noon in Calcutta when the sun is rising in Scotland.

Today there is no problem at all. Weather reports flash in a moment from country to country. The whole world cooperates in the making of weather maps. There are weather offices at thousands of places, and weather is observed in them around the clock, seven days a week. In some places the observations are taken every hour, at others every six hours.

In the middle of the night a lonely observer in Duluth, for example, goes out to look at the weather and the instruments. But he is comforted by the thought that thousands of observers in other places are going out at the same time. In Calcutta it is near noon, and

When the sun sets in the Bering Sea, it is midnight in Duluth.

the observer goes out in the heat and glaring sunshine. At the same time it is cold in Glasgow where the sun is rising as a Scotchman goes out to look at the clouds. Across from Alaska, beyond the Bering Sea the sun is going down. There are patches of snow here and there and a cold fog is coming in as a Russian observer looks in the instrument shelter. On a ship in the Mediterranean a Norwegian officer goes out on deck to take an observation at sunrise.

Within the hour all these observations and thousands of others will be on the weather maps in Juneau, Paris, Tokyo, Rome, Chicago and many other cities. For the

Predicting the Weather

fact that all these people speak different languages makes no problem at all. Weather is international. It has a special language of its own. The weather reports are sent in numerals in an international code. They are drawn on maps in the same figures and symbols in all countries. A weather map drawn in Turkey, Japan, India, Russia, Mexico, Sweden and all other countries looks and reads the same as a weather map drawn in the United States or Canada.

To see how maps are drawn, let us take an imaginary trip to the Weather Bureau in Washington, D. C. It is two o'clock in the morning. A damp, cold wind has been blowing from the northeast. It is getting colder. There is a gust of wind, and rain spatters against

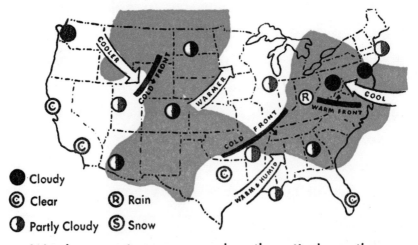

● Cloudy
Ⓒ Clear   Ⓡ Rain
◑ Partly Cloudy   Ⓢ Snow

Weather maps in newspapers show the nation's weather.

the side of the old red brick building as we go in.

Inside we find thirty men and women working on maps. Some of them are in uniform of the Air Force and Navy. For this is a joint process. The maps go to Weather Bureau offices, Navy ships at sea, and Air Force bases. The people here work fast around the clock. A new shift of workers comes on every eight hours.

In a small room a battery of machines is writing reports received by wire from all over North America, and by radio from ships at sea and from Europe and Asia. Pages of reports are taken from the machines and carried to the maps, where they are quickly put down in figures and symbols. Every station shown on the map is represented by a circle—a white circle if the sky there is clear, partly black if the sky is partly clouded, black if the sky is all covered with clouds. Symbols around the circles show the direction of the wind at that spot, its velocity, the temperature of the air, dew point, visibility, the kind of clouds if any, and the ceiling. They also indicate the air pressure and how it has changed during the past three hours. And they tell a good deal about precipitation. They tell how much there was during the last six hours, whether rain or snow is falling now, and when it began.

Predicting the Weather

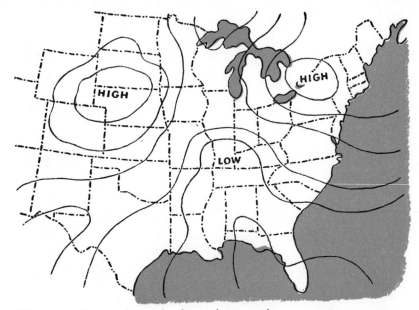

Lines are drawn through places having the same air pressure.

We stop beside a meteorologist who is drawing black lines on a map. He tells us that the lines pass through places that have the same air pressure. He points to several areas around which he has drawn a line.

"These are the Highs and Lows," he says. "The Highs," he explains, "are regions where the air pressure is high. In such places there is generally clear weather. The air is gently settling downward. It is blowing outward from the center and around the High, turning in the same direction as the hands of a clock go. The High

How the air circulates around the Highs and Lows.

is cool or cold, especially on the east side where the winds are from the north or northwest."

"And the Lows?" we ask.

"The Lows are regions where the air pressure is low. In such places we usually see cloudy weather—rain in summer and rain or snow in winter. In general, the Low covers a region where the air is being pushed upward. The air is blowing into and around a center. In the United States this means that warm air from the south is blowing into the east side of the Low. Cool or cold air from the north is coming into the west side.

"Highs and Lows," the meteorologist goes on to say, "don't stand still except now and again for a few hours. You can see them moving across the maps every day. Nearly every Low is followed by a High and then another Low. Our weather comes to us from the west, and the Highs tend to move from northwest to southeast. They often change direction. But in nearly all cases the final result is the same. The Highs appear first on the border of the United States in the west or northwest, and they leave the country in the east or northeast."

We notice that the meteorologist has marked a Low center in Georgia. "What is going to happen to that Low?" we ask.

"That Low is going to move up the eastern seaboard," he says. "Before morning our rain in Washington here will change to snow."

"Will it?" we wonder and move on to look at another map. We are puzzled by some heavy colored lines on it and ask about them.

"These heavy lines show the *fronts*," a meteorologist explains. "They are the boundaries between masses of warm air and masses of cold air moving into regions where pressure is low. The fronts are the most exciting places on the map. You know how it is on a war front where two armies are drawn up—there is bound to be conflict. That's how it is at a front on the map. If we could always guess what will happen there, we would be able to forecast the weather much better."

The meteorologist is saying something every weather forecaster will agree with. For most of the bad weather and the principal changes in weather happen along the fronts. *Air masses* are the chief actors in the drama of weather. Beside them Highs and Lows play secondary parts.

But what are air masses? Where do they come from? Why do they act as they do? And what exactly is it that happens at a front?

We are really getting to the heart of the weather problem when we ask these questions. To understand air masses and how they behave is to understand some of the biggest things in meteorology.

An air mass isn't just *any* body of air. It is a very large body—1,000 miles or more across, perhaps—having more or less the same temperature and moisture throughout. This is what makes it different.

How did the air mass get that way? By staying sev-

Predicting the Weather

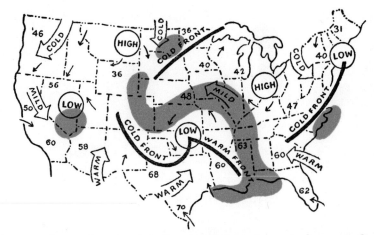

This map shows the weather for April first. Arrows show air flow; blue areas show rainfall; numbers give temperature.

eral days in one place. If it was "bred" over a warm ocean, the air mass will be warm and moist. If it was "bred" over a cold land, it will be cold and dry.

In our country the warm air masses move in from the southeast, the south and southwest. Most of them have come across southern waters and so are moist. They move in ahead of a Low.

Our cold air masses come down from northern waters and the cold regions of Canada. They move in north and west of the Low center.

Somewhere on the map these warm and cold currents are sure to come together. Like oil and water they will not mix easily. Each will keep itself to itself. What will happen?

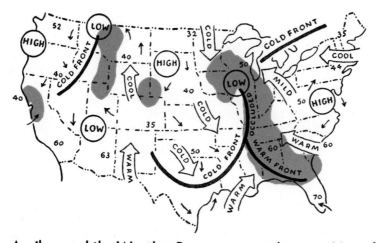

On April second the Weather Bureau put out this map. Note the changes since April first as shown on the map on page 114.

Perhaps the warm air mass will advance against a cold air mass. The warm air will push upward and blow over the top of the cold air. The front between the two air masses will then be called a *warm front*. Because the warm air has climbed up high over the cold air, clouds will form ahead of the warm front for perhaps a hundred miles or more. Rain and snow are likely to fall. They will keep on falling till the front passes.

Perhaps, on the other hand, a cold air mass will advance against the warm air mass. Being heavier, the cold air will nose under the warm air and push it up. All along the edge of the cold air where it is pushing under the warm air will be what we call a *cold front*. Here, too, clouds are likely to form. There may be rain or snow.

Predicting the Weather

Sometimes for a while there may be very little motion at a front. Then it is called a *stationary front*. Sometimes, again, a conflict takes place not between a warm and a cold air mass but between two cold air masses. It happens because cold fronts move faster than warm fronts. The cold air that is nosing under warm air at a cold front may catch up with the cold air over which the warm air is climbing at a warm front. All the warm air in this part of the Low has left the ground, and so at the ground two masses of cold air are left pushing against each other. One is nearly always colder than the other and noses under it. We have then what is called an *occluded* front. On an occluded front bad weather is very likely.

Knowing about air masses makes the Low on the map much more understandable. We begin to see that a Low is not just a whirl of air around a center of low pressure as it seemed when we saw the meteorologist marking it on the map. It is a battleground where air masses come together on fronts and wrestle with one another.

Now we hear the meteorologist who explained the heavy front lines to us say that if we watch the sky and the wind, we can see signs of the fronts approaching.

"Far out in advance of the Low center," he says, "you will have cool and clear weather. But pretty soon you will see thin, white clouds high up. These are cirrus clouds, made of ice crystals. They are in the stream of air which left the ground near the Low center. They have been carried far ahead, rising above the cool air. As the Low comes nearer, the warm air is closer to the ground. You will see clouds lower down in the sky now. Precipitation will begin.

"After the warm front passes, you will notice that the wind will change. The rain or snow will stop. But the air will still be moist and usually the sky will be partly cloudy. Now and then there may be a brief shower. The cold front will be just beyond the horizon. You will see it marked by a line of heaped-up clouds, often by long lines of thunderstorm clouds. When the front passes, you will notice a sudden shift of wind and a quick drop in temperature. Often there will be a hard squall, a thunderstorm and heavy showers. But the rain is soon over and the sky behind the cold front clears."

He shows us tonight's maps of the upper air which, he says, have been drawn from observations made by pilot balloons and radiosondes.

"These are prognostic maps," he says, showing us a file of maps of the past week. "Prognostic maps are maps of the weather expected tomorrow. Most of them proved to be correct, but there are a few mistakes. Weather prediction is not perfect, of course. There are lots of things we need to know about the weather, lots of problems we haven't solved yet. We are constantly looking for the answers."

We step over to take a look at a machine which copies maps and sends them on a wire to weather offices. This machine is called a *facsimile*.

"That's a great labor saving device," we hear someone say. "Today most weather offices use reports by wire to draw their own maps of weather over the whole country. Some day nearly all the local weather offices will use maps sent out from Washington by facsimile. It is a new thing being introduced as fast as possible. When local offices can get weather maps by facsimile, they won't have to make many maps of their own."

It is 4 o'clock when we leave the building. The rain has turned to snow. We are feeling the strong winds blowing around the Low. The weather forecast this time was pretty good.

11.

Weathermen in Action

Everybody talks about the weather. A great many people with all sorts of instruments and without any instruments at all are observing it. Now let us see what the local weather offices do with the information they get. We will take a flying trip to a few of them and see how the different regional needs in different parts of the country are taken care of.

Our first stop is New York City. The offices, we find, are up on the 29th floor of a building in a section called the Battery, at the lower tip of Manhattan. We thought perhaps we should see people making maps here. But we find that in this office very few maps are made. Here they get facsimile maps from Washington and make their forecasts from these.

New York's special problem, the meteorologist tells us, is countless inquiries. Many thousands of people want to know what the weather will be. Maps and forecasts printed in the newspapers, announcements on radio and television aren't enough. New Yorkers want the important question of what the weather is going to do answered by telephone. Naturally the weather office can't handle all the calls one at a time. To do that it would need 200 telephones and hundreds of people to answer them 24 hours a day. It has solved its problem by robot phones.

"Every hour," the meteorologist explains, "the office sends a fresh forecast on a teletypewriter to the telephone central. There a girl operator records the forecast on a magnetic tape. Anybody in New York can pick up the receiver any time of the day or night, dial WE 6-1212, and hear the girl's voice give the latest forecast. The robot answers 30 to 50 thousand calls a day. How many depends on the weather. The record, I believe, is 374,781 calls in one day."

Our visit to the office comes near the end of a hot spell, and people are worn out with the heat. Everybody is wanting to know when there will be a break in the heat wave. It really is unbearably hot. At one o'clock in the afternoon the temperature is 94°. Thousands of calls are coming to the robot. A break has been predicted because this morning there is a weak cold front in upstate New York and eastern Pennsylvania. The sky is cloudless. If the cold front fails to reach the city, it will be the hottest day of the year.

"It will surely reach us this afternoon—be here at the Battery about ten minutes after three," the meteorologist says. "Come and look at the radar."

We go over to the radar screen, and near its edge we see a line of white patches.

"Those are the echoes from thunderstorms on the cold front," he says. "Watching the echoes move on the radar, we get a good idea of the time the rain will reach New York. The observations help us a lot with the forecasts by telephone robot, radio and television. Over at La Guardia airport they make forecasts, too. They predict the weather and make radio broadcasts for the big planes crossing the Atlantic and for other aircraft, of course, commercial and private. We pick up the La Guardia broadcasts and send them out from here, because they carry farther from this tall building. Airports all around this area tune in on them to get the latest weather. In that way pilots get the forecasts and reports they want even when office phones are busy."

Then we go up on the roof to see the weather instruments up there. At twenty minutes after three we hear a roll of thunder. We see black clouds in the west and the white towers and high anvils of thunderstorm clouds. Lightning flashes constantly. As the city darkens, lights go on in thousands of offices. But the warning has gone out, and the power company has reserve power ready for the drain on the lighting system.

Lights go on when an afternoon thunderstorm strikes New York.

At twenty-eight minutes after three a great, ragged squall cloud spreads darkly across lower Manhattan. The gale begins. Cool air roars around the building as a few big drops of rain fall. We leave the roof after noting on the thermograph that at three o'clock the temperature reached 98°. Relief came to the Battery just 18 minutes later than the time predicted. The temperature is down to 82° now. It is going down slowly. It takes time for the city's great masses of stone, brick, and concrete to cool off.

But now let us change scene, time and weather. Suppose we are in Cincinnati. It is early spring. Days of warm rain and melting snow have poured vast amounts of water into the Ohio. The river is in flood. Flood control works have helped some, but things are still critical. The crew in the weather office work around the clock, talking to the engineers, putting out bulletins, making weather forecasts. The engineers are worried. Right now the skies are clear. Things would look hopeful if it weren't for the teletype machines, which bring a disturbing story. The forecaster says the flood will get worse.

Overhead, streamers of cirrus clouds begin to write a message across the sky. Later we see a halo around

123

the sun—the light rays have been bent on passing through the ice crystals. We see the clouds lowering, telling us the same story as the teletype machines. A warm front and more rain are coming to the Ohio Valley. Noon arrives amid heavy rain clouds and gathering darkness. The sun is barely seen. Before nightfall light rain begins.

The office sends out warning after warning that the river will rise to still higher stages. There is much anxiety, for higher water spells a lot of misery for a lot of people.

By morning there is steady, heavy rain over all the upper valley. The weathermen are too busy to talk to us. But we get a look at the latest maps in the office and see that the rising waters of the Ohio are only part of the weather story.

In the rear of the Low a big High and cold air mass have pushed down from Canada into the Northern Rockies. The High is spreading eastward into the Dakotas and Nebraska. A strong cold front swings down the mountains and across the plains with snow, high winds and temperatures very low for this time of year.

We forget the flood for a moment. We realize that a hundred other problems must be handled as the cold wave pours into the country. The teletype reports in the Cincinnati office bring some of the problems close.

We see that forecasts of cold weather are broadcast in western States with the words "Notify stockmen!"

The stockmen to whom the weathermen refer are sheep herders mainly. In the West 27 million sheep feed on open ranges. Melting snows in the spring bring out

Heavy rainfall may cause rivers and streams to flood.

Weathermen in Action

Stockmen are warned of a sudden drop in temperature.

fresh grass in higher places in the mountains. To these higher ranges millions of sheep are driven along the trails. And up there they have no protection except in ravines, behind cliffs and in the woods. So in the spring the weathermen always have to be on the lookout, especially as lambs are born on the open range—a sudden cold snap without warning will cause heavy losses. The words "Notify stockmen!" are full of meaning. As the cold winds cut down the slopes, millions of sheep—and cattle, too—will be moved as quickly as possible to any shelter that can be found.

We see nothing on the teletype about the deep South. At this time of year weathermen are not afraid that the cold wave will move down far enough to damage fruit groves in the far South. In the spring the big Highs and cold waves seldom do much damage in the deep South.

It is in winter that the trouble occurs. In winter the cold waves that come with huge Highs and strong cold fronts sometimes reach to the Gulf Coast and into Florida or to southern California. When the cold threatens to do that, the weathermen get busy. They send out warnings. Sometimes they succeed in saving millions of dollars to fruit growers. When the warnings come, the orchardists get out their five- or ten-gallon pots, fill them with fuel, set them up between the rows of trees, and light smoky fires. The lower air gets warm. It mixes with the air above to about the height of the treetops. Only a thin layer of air near the ground gets really cold. The heaters warm this layer and keep the freeze out of the orchards.

Weathermen have a big responsibility when they advise that fires be lighted in the orchards. For only when the conditions in the air are just right will fires be needed. Otherwise, costly fuel will just be wasted.

So far as Florida is concerned, however, it has a worse enemy than occasional winter frosts. That enemy is the hurricane. Let us, therefore, transfer ourselves to the Miami Weather Bureau and see what happens when a hurricane is located.

Weathermen in Action

We find that the Miami Weather Bureau has a special office for hurricane warnings. It is to this office that reports from ships and islands in the Caribbean region come. As soon as a hurricane is reported, the office maps it and observes the path it is taking. The Air Force and Navy help. They send planes into the hurricane area to find and report where the storm's center is. Sometimes the planes fly directly into the storm center.

In the warm regions near the equator, hurricanes move from east to west. But when they come northward into our latitudes, they usually turn around and go eastward in the belt of west winds. As they approach islands and coasts, the weather office sends out warnings.

No time is wasted then. People in the hurricane region board up the windows in stores and homes. Plate glass store windows are very costly. And home owners know from bitter experience that if the winds get into any opening such as a broken window, they are liable to take the roof off and wreck the building. Anybody who is in a place of danger on the coast knows, too, that he may have to leave at short notice and he gets ready for that. As many as 50,000 people have been brought inland in advance of one of these great storms.

We have come to the office at an exciting time. For

A hurricane can tear off the roof and wreck a building.

Weathermen in Action

Pairs of red flags with black centers are hurricane warnings.

four days a great hurricane has been moving slowly across the Caribbean. Day and night the reports from islands, ships and planes have been written on the maps. A center of low pressure marking the position of the hurricane has been watched, and warnings have been sent by radio to ships and islands in its path. Very few reports are coming in from ships now. On getting the warnings, they ran away from the path of the storm.

The Weather Bureau office in Miami is in a penthouse on top of a tall building. We can see over the city and far out where the Atlantic Ocean disappears in the haze on the horizon. A hot wind blows in gusts. Near by we see palm trees swaying in the wind and hear the sound of hammers as people board up windows. Square red flags with black centers fly in pairs from towers and poles along the coast.

Everybody knows the flags are hurricane warnings.

We see a weatherman go to one of the teletypewriter machines and send two messages. One is to the Navy base. One is to the Air Force base. The Navy agrees to send a plane into the storm this morning. The Air Force will send one from the base in Bermuda in the afternoon. Brave men will battle violent winds and hunt for the calm center of the great storm.

There is a row of microphones in the office, with lines running to all the radio and television stations in

A Navy plane hunts the calm center of a great storm.

Weathermen in Action

Miami and to stations in other cities of Florida. The weatherman now pushes a button, and he is on the air. His words go into every part of Florida. He tells the people just what the hurricane is doing, how strong the winds are, and how much tide there will be on the coast when the storm center arrives.

While we wait for a report from the Navy plane, we learn that teletypewriter machines are carrying messages around the coast from southern Texas to Massachusetts. For even up in New England people become anxious when a hurricane is reported. Ever since 1938 when a storm struck New England and did more than a quarter of a billion dollars' worth of damage, people there have been nervous about hurricanes.

In a little while we hear that a message has arrived from the Navy plane. It is right in the "eye" of the storm. The crew found it by looking in the radar. Battered by terrific winds, the plane has reached its objective, and now crew members have figured out their position. Naturally it is also the location of the storm center. Later the Air Force plane sends another report. The hurricane is getting closer.

When the hurricane comes within the scope of their radar, the weathermen at the office watch the echoes.

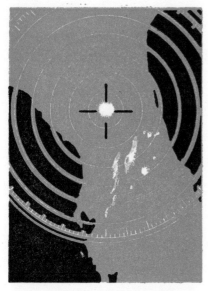

11:00 p.m. August 26

5:00 a.m. August 27

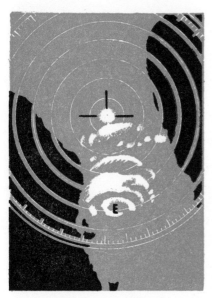

6:30 a.m. August 27

9:30 a.m. August 27

The hurricane of August 26-27, 1949, as it appeared on the radar-scope. E marks the eye of the storm.

Weathermen in Action

We go over and take a look at the radar, too. White spiral bands show on the screen. There is a small dark spot where the "eye" of the storm has no rain to send echoes. From now until the hurricane roars across the coast and moves up the state, the center will be seen by radars at Miami and other places.

"Do you expect much damage from the storm?" we ask the weatherman.

"To property, yes," he answers. "But so far as human life is concerned, we don't have to worry. We don't have much loss of life nowadays when a hurricane comes. Our warnings make all the difference in the world. Before the hurricane service had these modern methods, hundreds and thousands of lives used to be lost in a single storm. Now it is rare that a hurricane takes as many as a dozen lives. Generally in recent years only one or two people have been lost. And they were killed mostly by falling electric wires or because they ventured out into the storm when they should have stayed in a safe place."

We are impressed. We go away feeling somehow proud of man. The forces of Nature are so big and often so hostile. And yet, though he cannot control them, man can and does protect himself from them.

12.

For the Benefit of All

Not long ago a farmer, named George W. Richards, traveled to Washington from Minnesota. He came on the invitation of the United States Government, which wanted to honor him for helping the Weather Bureau understand the weather.

This man was eighty years old. When he was a lad of twenty, the Government had given him a rain gauge and a shelter box with thermometers. It had given him these instruments in exchange for a promise—that he would keep a daily record of the weather in his home town of Maple Plain, Minnesota. For sixty years George Richards had kept his promise. Day in, day out, during all those sixty years he had recorded the weather in his home town. He received no pay at all for this service. All he got was the satisfaction of doing something useful.

In Washington George Richards shook hands with high officials who had met to do him honor. He didn't in the least realize that *he* was the important person there. But the government people looked at him with admiration and with something of envy. What a grand parade of weather this man with the pleasant smile and quick step had seen in sixty years! Violent storms had passed before him, great cold waves and blizzards, heavy rains, crashing hail, deep snow, blistering heat. Through it all he had faithfully kept the records. Every single day he had made a note of any up and down in the weather in Maple Plain, Minnesota. Put all together, his records gave the people of the whole country a very good idea of the climate in his part of America.

George Richards didn't think he had done anything wonderful. "I've enjoyed it," he said. "When you watch weather close like that, it's exciting."

This faithful record keeper wasn't the only person

the Government wanted to honor. Lots of other people had kept voluntary records for a very long, long
time. Five others had kept it just as long as he had, but
for reasons of health or business hadn't been able to
travel to Washington. Several others had kept records
for fifty-five years. Some had done it for fifty. And a
great many had been at it more than forty years.

For though most of us aren't aware of it, the United
States has a small army serving it without pay. About
5,000 men and women are keeping daily records of the
weather in their own part of the country on a volunteer
basis. Each is building up a local weather picture. Out
of all the pictures in these little pieces of America, we
get a grand picture of the climate in all parts of our
vast country.

There was a time when the Weather Service knew
much less about climate than they do today. That was
back in 1870 when Congress first set up a national
weather service. At that time a great many people were
seeking homesteads in little known parts of the West.
They had to know what sort of climate they were moving into. Would they be able to raise wheat there? Or
was the climate right for corn? What kind of house
would they have to build? Were the winters long and

hard? Would settlers be likely to encounter drought?

So the Government asked for volunteer record keepers. In time it got a staff of paid observers, too. For it's not fun to keep the records in all of the places the Government wants to know about.

In Death Valley, California, for instance, the summer heat is nearly the worst in the world. Once it went up to 134°, the second highest record in the world. At Greenland Ranch in Death Valley the *average* July

In Death Valley, summer heat is nearly the worst in the world.

temperature is above 100°. At the hottest time of day in the middle of summer it averages 116°. Here a volunteer observer kept records for years. In the hottest weather he had to lie still on a wet sheet in front of a big fan. Today there is a resort there, a big air-conditioned hotel, and an airport.

On the summit of Mt. Washington in New Hampshire, paid observers suffer extremes of weather of a different sort. The wind up there reaches speeds un-

On Mt. Washington, wind velocity can be 231 miles an hour.

known anywhere else in the country. The wind record there is 231 miles an hour. The weather station has to be tied to the solid rock of the mountain by steel cables; otherwise in these big winds the station might take off like a rocket ship. In winter the winds leave ice on the weather station like frost around the freezing unit in a refrigerator—only there are tons of ice. The wind gauge up on the ice-encrusted tower has to be heated by electricity to keep it from freezing stiff. The observers don't venture outside in winter unless they have to. They value their lives too much. Some daring men who have tried to climb the mountain in the winter have been frozen in the bitter gales that sweep the slopes. The trails are marked here and there by their gravestones.

Besides being interested in climate, the Weather Service was very much concerned about the safety of ships. Storms on the Great Lakes and the seacoasts were wrecking hundreds of ships, and the Government was determined to stop it. Storm warnings were badly needed. To get information about storms the Weather Service established weather stations in all sorts of places. And it found the right people to stay in them and observe the weather. It takes courage to stay in some of the places. One station stands off the northwest corner

The weather station on Tatoosh Island is a lonely spot.

of the United States on a rock called Tatoosh Island. The great storms sweeping eastward from the vast Pacific Ocean hurl wind, rain, and heavy seas at the

lonely post. But lonely or not, the observer stays and
keeps the records. Without his messages to the main-
land many a ship would be wrecked on the rocky coast
or sunk in the open sea.

Ship owners, sea captains, crews, and even ordinary
passengers are mighty grateful for the warnings, you
may be sure. And the number of ships wrecked has
dwindled to a very few. At the same time people have
found many other uses for the Weather Service. Farmers
found it so helpful that in 1891 the Weather Service
became the Weather Bureau in the Department of
Agriculture.

Today the Bureau is part of the Department of Commerce. For business, industry, and transportation have
come to depend on the weatherman even more than
farmers do. Especially has this been so since the de-
velopment of aviation. Every year there are more planes
in the sky. Every year more people travel by air. Every
year aviation makes greater demands on the weatherman.

Of course, for the pilot of an airplane the weather
reports are more important than for anyone else—the
distance he makes depends on the winds in upper levels.
He must know on which level he can make the best
time, and how he can avoid dangerous conditions. But

he gets many weather information services besides. Whether he is on the ground or in the air, teletypewriter and radio bring him news of the latest weather. He can get information and advice almost instantly. Then, too, many pilots make a habit of calling at a weather office to look at the maps and the latest weather reports along the route. They insist on fresh reports. Even from distant places a report is considered of little value by pilots if it is more than two hours old. For planes move swiftly, and the weather is constantly moving and changing. The combination is difficult, yet weathermen meet its demands.

What the Weather Bureau finds out it makes available to all the people who need the information for any reason at all. And it constantly tries to improve ways of reporting and forecasting the weather.

We know a great deal about weather today. We have traveled far since the days when people thought rain came down through openings in the firmament or that lightning was a thunderbolt thrown by angry Zeus. We have gone way beyond predicting weather from old weather signs and sayings.

Weather prediction is pretty good now. Yet it could be better. Weathermen believe it will be a lot better.

For the Benefit of All

They hope—yes, expect—that *electronic brains*, or educated robots, will one day take over a lot of the work weathermen struggle over today. We saw how the telephone and radio robots already have solved some of their service problems. In the last few years electronic brains have been built that may solve the most difficult weather problems, even in all the important details observed and measured in the free air. Perhaps some day we will get our weather predictions from a machine. If and when we do, weathermen will have achieved another victory in a long line of victories over the invisible ocean that is our atmosphere.

Index

Index

Index